Writing Business Decision Papers

A Comprehensive How-To Guide

I0569025

Erwin Martinez

Writing Business Decision Papers: A Comprehensive How-To Guide

Copyright © 2024 Erwin Martinez

Paperback ISBN: 978-1-963732-06-1
Hardcover ISBN: 978-1-963732-07-8

Published By

The Publishing Pad
www.thepublishingpad.com

Disclaimer

Table of Contents

Preface

Why I Wrote This Guide

The idea of writing this book grew out of 42 years of experience I have writing and, most influentially, coaching others on how to write important documents in business. These documents included a variety of papers that could be summarized as being *decision papers*. They were created to effect major changes, solve problems, seize opportunities, change strategic directions, launch new services or products, implement new technologies, or evaluate what could be learned from major events or projects. They always resulted in recommendations to commit large amounts of money and scarce and strategic resources to execute the recommendations. Many times I had to live with the approved outcomes of these papers in the form of projects and initiatives that executed the papers' recommendations. I managed or oversaw the projects. I was a member of and chaired the executive steering committees providing governance over these strategic projects.

At the front end of these 42 years was 15 years in systems integration consulting, followed by 27 years as an IT executive in various companies—including 24 years as a Chief Information Officer. I worked in multiple industries, although the majority of my experiences are in banking. I always took a "hands-on" approach to these papers. I either wrote them myself or reviewed them very closely, resulting in recommendations and directions to make changes. I also presented these papers to executive teams, CEOs, and boards.

As I coached others in the preparation of decision papers, what evolved was a standard set of practices and recommendations I would offer to those I was coaching. I knew if I ever could devote the time to it, I could turn all the advice I doled out at work into a comprehensive guide that can be universally understood and used by anyone. This is that guide.

Author Credentials and Background

My 42 years of experience include direct responsibility for writing business decision papers and for creating, maintaining, and enforcing the standards of these papers. Often I performed this work as part of being directly responsible for the company's Project Management Office (PMO) and Information Technology and Cyber Security functions. Many times I led classroom training on writing decision papers; usually preparing the training materials myself.

I have published articles (as the sole author) in several educational and professional publications, including MIT Sloan Management Review, Project Management Institute's Project Management Journal, Canadian Institute of Corporate Director's Director Journal, and Technology Review.

I have spoken at numerous conferences, including Bank Security Summit, Project Management Institute's Annual Conferences, by invitation at the Stanford Graduate School of Business, Canadian Ferry Association, and others.

I have a Bachelor of Arts degree in Administrative Sciences from Yale University, New Haven, Connecticut. I have Directors Certificate (ICD.D) from the Institute of Corporate Directors and The SFU Beedie School of Business in Vancouver, British Columbia. I have been recognized by the Hispanic IT Executive Council as of the "Top 100 Hispanics in Information Technology."

How This Guide Differs From All Others

<u>Written By a Practitioner</u>. I humbly present this guide from the perspective of a practitioner—not an academic, not an observer, not a no-skin-in-the-game consultant. That is just one key way this guide differs from others. I expect all of you reading this guide are also practitioners, or looking to be one. This book is written from one practitioner to another.

<u>Addresses Organizational Politics</u>. As you read, you will notice I continually revisit the topic of how to deal with bad, destructive politics that emerges in most organizations when there is a research and change process underway, such as with decision papers. This also comes from firsthand experience. I found that it was equally challenging getting the content and recommendations right as it was dealing with the inappropriate and underhanded ways detractors and saboteurs operated to undermine that very work. I would be remiss if I did not bring this to the surface and discuss such bad politics and detractors. That is the second way this guide differs from others. Politics in all its ugly manifestations is dealt with explicitly.

<u>Usage Cases Throughout</u>. This guide includes four fictionalized case studies that nonetheless are based on actual decision paper situations. The cases are described in the introduction and referred to throughout the text. This provides a real-world way to draw on examples as this book dispenses decision paper writing guidance. That is the third way this guide differs from others: usage of cases throughout.

<u>Advice Founded on Experience</u>. Like many of you, I wrote, edited, reviewed, and approved decision papers in the context of doing my job. I created, presented, and defended the content of these papers. I dealt with criticism, both constructive and inappropriate. The fourth way this guide differs from others is that each and every piece of advice included in the book came about from actual practice. You can decide whether the advice is useful or not. But, at a minimum, it is coming from a place of real experience.

Intended Audience

I wrote this guide for everyone who is at times required to write a decision paper at work or for an organization. This guide will teach you how to write clear, concise decision papers that meet the needs of your situation. The guide will point out the many pitfalls when writing a decision paper to help you avoid them.

If you are terrible at writing decision papers, this guide will greatly improve your capabilities. If you are very good at writing decision papers, this guide will challenge you to achieve at a higher level.

This guide is also for those who commission the writing of decision papers. It will help explain why you never quite get what you are asking for. It will give you a basis on which to engage the author(s) you are chartering with the task of writing the paper.

This guide can also be used by those whose job it is to set the standards for the style and content of documentation at an organization. It can be incorporated (with proper attribution) into the style guide and formatting requirements dictated by your business.

I hope you find my practical and realistic perspective helpful to you in your job. That is the goal of this book.

Introduction

Why Bad Decision Papers Are a Problem

When you can't write clearly, you are not thinking clearly. As William Zinsser noted in his book about writing nonfiction, *On Writing Well*: "Clear thinking becomes clear writing; one can't exist without the other. It is impossible for a muddy thinker to write good English."[1] Ergo, paying attention to the quality of a decision paper improves the thoughtfulness and logic the authors apply to the subject and aim of the paper.

I got the idea of creating a guide on how to write business decision papers when I reviewed a planning document written by an otherwise competent, highly experienced, highly knowledgeable, very dedicated manager who nonetheless produced a written piece of garbage. Ken's[2] paper was almost unsalvageable. We had to go through each section, each sentence, and review fundamentals. The final product required hours of collaboration and multiple redrafts. It was so completely restructured and reworded that it bore only the slightest resemblance to the original draft. In my many years as an information technology consultant and executive for various companies, I have been through this exercise many, many times. For some reason, our highly valued managers cannot write a clear decision paper. Or, more to the point, our managers cannot write clearly at all.

But rather than just say the paper was garbage, let me list a few of the problems with the paper—problems that appear, to one degree or another, in the first drafts of just about every decision paper or business document I have seen in the last 25 years. These are presented in alphabetical order.

---

[1] William Zinsser, *On Writing Well, 30th Anniversary Edition* (New York: Collins, 2006), 8.

[2] The situation actually happened. There was indeed a single event that made me determined to write this guide. I changed the name to avoid needless conflict and/or embarrassment. I also changed some of the details, but this account still captures the essence of the event. At the time, I did discuss with "Ken" how completely off the mark his paper was.

- Acronyms. The author used acronyms and abbreviations that were well known to those who had worked in the business and technology area of the project but were completely meaningless to those who had not. For example, many people, even those who work in financial institutions, would not know what this sentence means: "Security concerns require the blocking of ACH Trans codes 27 and 37 during testing on core bank 150's clients." What this text is saying is that, to be safe, during the testing of the system to be implemented in the proposed project, we will not execute transactions that would withdraw money from actual clients' checking and savings accounts that are maintained on the bank's banking system. One sentence uses jargon and can only be understood by a select few. The other sentence uses plain English and effectively communicates the point.

- Boss Said So. The author seemed to note the CEO's purported opinion wherever possible. This is an area that may be interesting, but it induces a big "So what?" from the discerning reader. Those appropriately looking for a strong logical argument for investing company resources need something more than the equivalent of "Mom said."

- Bulk. Given the specific subject of the decision paper, it was very long, over 30 pages. I wondered: was the paper long because the subject area merited it, or was it long so that the author could meet some type of perceived "weight test" for important projects?

- Conflicting Numbers. Some detailed cost and human resource estimates were included as appendices. That is fine. The problem in this paper was that in the body of the document, there were references to costs and resources that did not match the numbers in the appendices. Also, terminology changed when referring to some costs in the body of the document compared to how they were listed in the appendices.

- Confusing Structure. Section headings and section content seemed to have only a loose relationship to each other. For example, the Scope section included items that were actually background, risks, constraints, or objectives, and the Constraints section had nothing in it that could be fairly called a constraint.

- <u>Cut and Paste</u>. Certain sections were much longer than others and written in a different style with different wording when compared to the rest of the paper. It was clear to me that they had been lifted whole from other documents. There is nothing wrong and much right with using existing materials (with proper attribution when necessary) to make writing the paper more efficient. But this cannot be done carelessly such that the reader is confused.

- <u>Formatting Problems</u>. There were seemingly random formatting problems. For example, section headings were sometimes in boldface and sometimes not, bulleted lists did not align, the table of contents did not match the actual content of the report, and within some paragraphs, font and text size changed for no reason.

- <u>Incompleteness</u>. Some sections did make sense but were clearly not complete. Complex projects, for example, face many risks. Yet the Risk section of the paper listed only a few risks, all of them technical in nature. Clearly a complex and large project, which was the scope of this document, would have more than a few risks, and the risks would stretch beyond technology to include the business process, vendors, users, clients, schedule, security, etc.

- <u>Maddening Politeness</u>. The author seemed to have an overarching desire not to offend anyone in any way. It was very difficult to understand items such as the business case for making the investments and improvements called for in the paper. The author felt he could not write the truth, which was that the current system was lacking necessary features, that it was uncompetitive, and that clients dissatisfied with the system had already left, taking their business to our competitors—all as a result of dissatisfaction with the product. Instead, euphemistic jargon was used, such as "desire to leverage more advanced features," "take the product set to the next level," and "better serve key client bases." By being overly polite, the author had thwarted the goal of clearly explaining powerful and compelling reasons to fund and execute the project.

- <u>Mysterious Timelines</u>. When did some of the key events mentioned in the paper occur? If approval was received, when would the project start? Who knows, since neither of these items was addressed clearly in the paper.

- <u>No Background</u>. The paper started with a discussion of the project's objectives. A section on project objectives is indeed necessary for such a document. However, it should have started with some sections that let the reader know relevant history, where this project came from, and why it was being presented at that time. These are often addressed with sections called "Document Purpose" and "Background." Without such sections, many readers will be lost from the start.

- <u>Nomenclature Inconsistency</u>. Positions, systems, teams, and departments were referred to in what appeared to be a random set of ways. Was the sponsoring department "Electronic Banking," "eBanking," or "Treasury eProducts"? There was no way to tell that these terms all referred to the same department. There were similar problems when references were made to existing systems, vendors, and regulators.

- <u>Passive Voice</u>. Business writers often overuse passive voice such that it is difficult or even impossible to identify the "who" behind key decisions and viewpoints. The reader is unnecessarily confused when we say, "A decision was made to exclude the incumbent vendor due to perceptions that competitor products may better serve our needs." Who made this decision: the IT Department? The IT Department and the business owners? Was the CEO involved? We can't tell.

- <u>Poor English</u>. The author was not adept enough to render clear expository writing. One had to read and reread sections to try to understand what the author intended to say. Paragraphs lacked topic sentences. Text sometimes did not match the content promised by section headings.

- <u>Sections Omitted</u>. Some very relevant topic areas were just ignored. This was another problem of (in)completeness. Were there technology dependencies? What methodology would be used in the proposed project? You couldn't tell because there were no sections to address these areas.

- <u>Typos</u>. The author did not proofread the paper, or, worse, the author's proofreading skills were so weak that obvious and distracting errors were left in the paper.

- <u>Unclear Purpose</u>. The paper was written for a specific purpose. It was a Business Case and Project Plan for a multimillion-dollar project. The paper was to go to various constituencies to explain the overall plan. Its purpose was to provide sufficient detail so that stakeholders and senior executives (some with little involvement in or knowledge of the project) could approve the startup of the project and provide preliminary approval for the project expenditures. (There were other purposes, too, but to simplify, let's leave it at that.) Nowhere in the first draft could you get a sense of why this document was written, nor what it was intended to achieve. Instead, it seemed to ramble from topic to topic and then abruptly stop.

- <u>Vague References</u>. Several times the author referred to an incident that, we were to believe, was well known. There apparently had been some type of systems outage or data quality problem. Since the author assumed that all readers would be aware of this incident, he did not describe it. Clearly, if the reader was not familiar with the incident, then he would be lost and, also importantly, a bit angry that he was seemingly deliberately being confused. Interesting and relevant historical incidents belong in a Background section.

I should add one other impetus for writing this guide. And it is a big one. Ken, like so many others that I have worked with over the years, seemed to be oblivious to these issues. Or, to quote William Zinsser's *On Writing Well* again, "few people realize how badly they write."[3]

This was just one of the many times I received a decision paper from a manager who handed it over without the slightest idea that it was indecipherable. Such authors have no idea that what they have rendered is not going to do whatever it is that they intended to accomplish by writing the paper in the first place. They might not even have a clear idea as to what they are trying to accomplish—which makes the bad situation even worse. I am no psychologist, but I have come to believe that many people who complain about being victims of politics, indecision, analysis paralysis, etc. are unwittingly contributing to this malaise in their organizations by providing decision papers that do not serve their desired purpose. The papers create more confusion than clarity. They create the illusion that work is getting done, decisions getting made.

---

[3] Zinsser, *On Writing Well*, 17.

What Is a Decision Paper?

I use the term "Decision Paper" as a shorthand way to describe the written product in situations where a document is needed to achieve an objective by laying out a logical story leading to one or more recommendations. A decision paper is written in an organizational setting, such as a business, a nonprofit, an academic institution, a religious institution, etc. Many people may read the document, either shortly after it is written or much later.

The following list describes some characteristics of what this guide calls a decision paper.

- Its purpose is to drive to a decision. This is the key differentiator between decision papers and other formal writing. A decision paper's reason for being is to spur action and/or effect change. A decision paper's purpose could be to:
  - Select an option among competing options
  - Stop a project, shut down a business, or end a product line
  - Approve a new project, business, or product line
  - Approve the next stage of an endeavor
  - Recommend improvements (incremental or large-scale) to learn from a particular failure
- It is read by a broad range of people. These include:
  - Those directly involved with the subject of the paper
  - Those will little to no prior knowledge of the subject of the paper
  - Auditors or regulators—those with a role of reviewing the soundness of the logic in the decision paper but with otherwise no interest in the ultimate decisions that are made
  - People from the very junior to the very senior; from the very technical to the very untechnical
- It will be read long into the future. Perhaps it will be read at a time when the original author or authors are no longer in the organization.

- It works through a complex situation and decision in an area of great consequence to the organization. If the situation were not complex and consequential, it would just be handled with a short memo.

- It involves factors and considerations that may not have been revealed yet or may not be well known. They need to be discovered, researched, and analyzed.

- There are often differing viewpoints about the facts, logic and conclusions described in the decision paper. These differing viewpoints will be settled once and for all by publishing the final decision paper.

- The situation calls for a logical, methodical recommendation. Or, stated in the negative, the situation would be ill-suited to a decision based on gut feeling, political power plays, mindless risk aversion, or extrapolation of past decisions.

- The facts, analyses, and decisions described in the decision paper require that it be *auditable*. For papers on important and consequential subjects, there is a certainty that it will be scrutinized and examined, perhaps by parties hostile or unreceptive to the facts, logic, and recommendations contained in the paper.

There are many documents one writes in an organizational setting that are not decision papers but nonetheless require clear writing. These could be, for example, meeting minutes, papers documenting the outcome of an experiment or test, research reports, product evaluations, etc. Generally, these *non-decision papers* describe important activity but do not drive toward a recommendation or conclusion. You will find many of the concepts in this guide to be useful in such endeavors. This guide, however, will focus solely on the development of excellent decision papers.

Note: This book is not about white papers written for marketing purposes. There are other books and articles that explore decision papers as primarily marketing tools to, for example, sell into other organizations. This guide does not include marketing white papers in the scope of the discussion. That is an entirely different kind of document. This guide considers decision papers as used internally within organizations (perhaps prepared with outside assistance) to drive focused action.

What Is Excellence in a Decision Paper?

There are a few characteristics of excellence in decision papers:

- <u>Answers All Questions</u>. The entire paper should answer any possible relevant and reasonable question that may arise. This is not just a matter of completeness, although completeness—completely covering all sections and topics—is essential to excellence. Answering all questions requires that you understand the paper's audiences or constituencies, fully anticipate their questions and curiosities, and include sufficient information and analysis to satisfy those needs.

- <u>Proceeds Logically</u>. The decision paper structure (a standard table of contents) is designed to build your story logically and sequentially. As readers step through an excellent decision paper, they see and understand how the work is unfolding. It makes sense to them.

- <u>No Sacred Cows</u>. The paper needs to tread in all areas that are relevant to the unfolding story of the decision paper. That some areas may be highly politically charged or politically protected does not change the fact they need to be included. It is fine to handle such sensitive topics with some care—but I advise including the sensitive topics fully where they are relevant to the paper. I will say more about this in the Methodology section discussion later in this guide.

- <u>Solution-Oriented</u>. Ultimately a decision paper presents a way forward in the sections titled "Alternatives" and "Recommendation." A decision paper cannot just be an exercise in analysis and thought. It must add value to the organization by laying out a way forward that thoughtfully and logically addresses the stated scope and objectives. The recommended way forward must provide real results and deal with underlying root causes and problems.

- <u>Act of Courage</u>. The decision paper's authors need to take the courageous steps of analyzing and recommending. It is usually politically easier to delay, off-load responsibility, and further analyze. In some company cultures, it is easier to just ask the CEO or equivalent organizational leader to make the key decisions and recommendations. But without courage on the part of the authors, there is little chance of reaching the best possible recommendation. As will be discussed later in this guide, sometimes you must have the courage to act, and other times you must have the courage to wait, to suspend action. You would suspend action not because you are scared or because it is easy, but because circumstances indicate that that is the most prudent step.

Organization and Structure of This Guide

This guide has an introduction (you are reading it now) and then three parts:

- Part 1: The Standard Decision Paper Structure. I propose a standard set of sections for every decision paper. I describe each section and what you would need to do to write it so that it is clear and concise. The sections are sequenced to logically build your argument. This standard structure can work in any industry, for any topic.

- Part 2: The ABCs of Writing a Decision Paper. This part addresses what you should and should not do when writing a decision paper. It is organized alphabetically by topic for ease of reference.

- Part 3: Now What? This part briefly recommends some ways to introduce the concepts and rules described in this guide to your own organization.

I use the following organizational methods and recurring sections throughout the book:

Bulleted Lists. You will notice that I make liberal use of bulleted lists. Those bulleted lists often begin with an underlined heading. Most often, those bullet headings are nouns or brief captions. This is a deliberate technique that can also be used well in decision papers. There are several reasons for this structure which (without any intended humor or irony) I will list in a bulleted list:

- Busy Reader. I am assuming that you, the reader, are busy. Very likely you are very busy. You may want to see what items you would like to read closely and what you would like to skim over. I want to make that as efficient as possible for you.

- <u>Referenceable</u>. Bulleted lists with brief, specific titles are easier to reference than a long series of paragraphs. When you read a document and later look for the text on the "Busy Reader," you have an easier chance of readily finding it in a bulleted list that has a simple title.

- <u>Independent Notions</u>. Many of the suggestions and thoughts in this guide, as with your decision papers, are independent of each other. In a series of paragraphs, this can seem like an endless litany of ideas. In a bulleted list, the separation between ideas is much clearer.

- <u>Hierarchical Notions</u>. Many suggestions and thoughts are hierarchical. Bulleted lists, with sub-bullets, are ideal for segregating the hierarchical notions in a way that naturally fits their structure.

<u>Means vs. Ends</u>. You will find throughout this guide discussion on whether a section or process pertains to the *means* or the *ends*. Decision paper authors should consider this nuance to be very important to understand. Some sections pertain to ends only, other sections pertain to means and ends. Here's what I mean:

- <u>Means</u>. This is the work undertaken to get to an outcome, a destination. In our case, this is the work *during* the preparation of the decision paper to develop and finalize the paper.

- <u>Ends</u>. This is the output, irrespective of the means. In our case, this is the work that comes *after* the decision paper is approved, funded, and supported to act on its recommendations.

For example, consider Scope. The scope of the *means* is the scope of the journey from preparing the decision paper all the way up to making recommendations. You will soon read that one of our cases is the Rivertown Plant Explosion where factory employee lives were lost in an accident. In the case of the Rivertown Plant Explosion, the *means scope* could include what documentation would be reviewed, who would be interviewed, whether fatal accident events at other companies would be examined, etc. The scope of the *ends* would include changes to equipment, equipment safety certification, organization structure, job duties and descriptions, equipment training, safety programs, etc.

<u>Political Misapplications</u>. In Part 1, I present a description of each of

the fifteen sections of a decision paper, what they are, what to include, and what to be aware of. For each of these, I also include a short sub-section entitled "Political Misapplications." This provides some warning and advice for dealing with the types of political trouble (such as sabo-tage) you can expect from those with less than pure motives as they try to prevent the work described in the decision paper from happening and/or work to discredit the authors and their recommendations.

Decision papers usually tread in areas of controversy, identify people and teams that have failed in some way, and advocate for changes that may or may not be welcomed. I would be remiss if I did not give explicit and prominent attention to the difficult people-politics that may emerge. In my experience, a lot of good and earnest work conducted by decision paper teams is undermined and sometimes destroyed in the gristmill of bad political actors. You need to be equally prepared for what goes into a good decision paper *and* how to deal with those up to no good who want to undermine your work.

Note that I do not mean to imply that all those who disagree with the decision paper development team or have other points of view are bad political actors. On the contrary, getting working drafts reviewed and being open to other recommendations or points of view is important and will make the decision paper product ultimately better. But I want to deal with a big challenge in decision papers: the reality that some people will do whatever they can, for selfish purposes, to undermine and stop the decision paper process from proceeding to a successful conclusion.

Cases Created for This Guide

I have created (concocted, really) four case studies that will be referred to throughout this guide as I illustrate concepts and sections of the decision paper with examples. Each of these cases is based on actual experiences I have had but is fictionalized with some details changed so that they are not the same as I experienced them. The cases are provided to make the guidance in this book easier to understand with the use of relatable examples.

- Failed Financial Systems Project. The scenario takes place at a midsized bank. A strategic and large-scale project was conducted to replace financial systems. The project failed. The project was substantially completed when it became clear that it would not meet the business needs and that the integration and user testing did not seem to have an end. Both testing phases were stopped when the project governance determined they were not making progress—every time a bug was fixed, it seemed at least one new bug was found. Ultimately the project was shut down, and usage of the old system continued. One of this decision paper's objectives is to solve a problem: Why did the Financial Systems project fail? Another is to seize an opportunity: What are the Lessons Learned? What near-term and long-term changes should be made to minimize the possibility of such an IT project failure in the future?

- Rivertown Plant Explosion. The scenario takes place at a single plant that is part of a large manufacturing business. Relatively new equipment was in use for a few months. One day, it inexplicably overheated and very shortly thereafter exploded. Six employees were killed, a dozen injured. Damage to the plant was in excess of 5 million dollars. The repair work to bring the plant back online and understand and fix the cause of the overheating and explosion is underway, but those matters are outside of the scope of the decision paper. This decision paper's primary objective is to review and validate the root cause analysis and determine near-term and long-term changes to implement so that this type of accident never occurs again. All options are on the table including shutting down the Rivertown Plant.

- Seattle Office Closing. The scenario takes place at a medium-sized professional services firm such as an engineering design or IT consulting firm. The firm has two large headquarters locations, one in San Francisco, California, and the other in Toronto, Ontario. The situation is that a new office location was opened in Seattle, Washington. Despite seeming to follow relevant processes, obtaining required signoffs and approvals, and having required documentation such as a business case, the office was a failure. It did not meet any of its targets in areas such as new clients, gross revenue, and net margin. It experienced much higher rates of employee turnover than those experienced at San Francisco or Toronto. After 24 months in operation, a decision was made to close the office. This decision paper's primary objective is to understand if anything went wrong with the company's new office process given what a clear failure the new Seattle office was. The paper will need to analyze and explain root causes and recommend near-term and long-term changes to policy and practice so that such a mistake is not made again.

- Strategy to Close the Lollipop Division. The scenario takes place at a large publicly traded corporate enterprise that produces and sells confections, sweets, and snacks. The primary outlet for their products is grocery stores. The enterprise has been in business for over a hundred years, with excellent brand identification and affinity with the public. One of its original products was its well-known line of multi-flavored lollipops. However, despite years of focus, attention, and innovation, the line's profitability and popularity have dropped steadily for the last 12 years. It no longer makes sense to continue the Lollipop Division given these business realities, despite it being considered part of the core corporate identity. This decision paper's primary objective is to create a strategy and plan for the orderly shutdown of the Lollipop Division. It will be important to shut down this product line while minimizing negative impacts to the brands and reputations of the remaining product lines. A secondary objective is to identify Lessons Learned from the failure to keep the Lollipop Division profitable and strategic—lessons that can be used by the existing product lines.

Getting Started

There are a few areas of focus that are essential to finalize before beginning the development of the decision paper.

- Richness of Source Material. The writers of a decision paper must be able to access diverse and pertinent source materials to make the process of reasoning through a paper worthwhile. Topics that lack sufficient information are frankly not yet ready for analysis. Such topics may be documented in a separate pre-decision-paper communication that asks for access to or creation of such source material. In some cases, bad power politics is at play where some political players would like to see the decision paper developed, but without making some pertinent facts and evidence available to the authors. If the source material is not available or will not be made available, then don't attempt to write the decision paper. Such an effort is bound to produce an incomplete and inadequate result.

- Team. It is essential that the right team be assembled and that they be given sufficient time and clear direction. Team composition should be cross-organizational in areas appropriate to the scope and objectives of the paper. Members should be chosen by their organizational executive leadership and/or the CEO. It is not unusual for a decision paper ad hoc team (let's call it "DPAH", and pronounce it "deeper") to have members join and/or drop off as the work gets underway. As long as this is to better address the scope and objectives as they are developed, this is a healthy step. Otherwise, it would be better to have stable team membership.

  While this guide does not get into issues of team dynamics (that is a big topic by itself), be mindful not to tolerate team members who engage in impolite, disrespectful, or disruptive behavior. Such team members should be jettisoned from the DPAH with little delay.

- Leadership. Leadership of the DPAH should be very clear and explicit. It is common and very effective, for example, to have two leaders from two major constituencies. Consider how effective it would be for the Failed Financial Systems Project DPAH group to be led jointly by a manager from Finance and a manager from IT. Sometimes joint leadership is with an employee and a consultant. I do not recommend self-directed teams for the DPAH; given the difficult tasks to be undertaken, this can easily devolve into analysis paralysis.

  Leaders must be skilled at facilitation—guiding and working with a diverse group of individuals. This skill is required of the leaders even if you employ expert facilitation, as is recommended in the next bullet point.

  Decision paper leaders must be willing to seize authority, have the courage to reason with and, if necessary, face down detractors, saboteurs, and others who get in the way of progress and change. For important decision paper topics, the leadership roles are not for the shy, timid, or faint of heart.

  And be wary of the political undermining that can result from placing the wrong person or persons in charge of the decision paper team. This is a common sneaky ploy to ultimately undermine the decision paper process. Look for the qualities of competence, courage, and independence in decision paper leadership assignments.

- Expert Facilitation. Decision paper development for large, strategic, and/or complex scopes can be greatly enhanced by unbiased expert facilitation. I view this largely as a function of complexity and size. For this to be effective, the facilitator must be both well skilled and truly independent. This may mean that, if there is a regular facilitator on staff at your organization, you steer clear of that individual in favor of someone with no biases or allegiances—whether perceived or real.

- Governance. Guidance and direction, i.e., governance, should come from the highest level possible. Highest level could mean the CEO (or equivalent) and/or the Board of Directors. This will help make sure the efforts and outputs of the DPAH are not buried and are taken seriously. More on this topic later in this guide.

- Timetable. A clear timetable should be set and widely communicated at the start of the decision paper development effort. This is admittedly not ideal, given that at the start of the decision paper exercise it is not clear how long it will take to conduct all the work. However, setting a firm timetable up front is important because if that is not done, political actors in the form of detractors and saboteurs may attempt to kill the decision paper initiative with a series of endless delays.

- "One-page" Charter. For the initiative to be started, it is best to have a one-page charter to establish the basic scope, objectives, budget, and schedule of the decision paper. Whether it is one or two or three pages is not as important as the point that it should be brief. The charter is not a substitute for the detailed work and documentation that will result from undertaking the decision paper development. It is enough information to authorize the conduct of the work.

   When writing the charter, avoid the temptation to preview or predict a possible or likely outcome to the decision paper process. For example, the Seattle Office Closing decision paper charter should not have a scope item worded as "review and correct flawed sales projection process." This assumes the outcome. "Review and recommend updates, if advisable, to the sales projection process" is more neutral, not presupposing the outcome.

- <u>DPAH Announcement</u>. In most modern organizations, a company-wide email with equivalent intranet posting would serve as the announcement of the formation of the Decision Paper Ad Hoc team. I recommend great care and attention be given to this communication. It should lay out a summary of the charter and clearly convey the organizational commitment to the process and the outcomes. For larger, more strategic areas of focus, this communication will be re-used later as others join and/or catch up on the importance of the decision paper.

- <u>Kickoff Meeting</u>. A Kickoff meeting with large representation across the organization can be an effective way to start the work. Parts of the agenda can be given to key leaders from across the organization to communicate the importance of the initiative and alignment of key leadership. However, some company cultures will view this step as an unnecessary waste given that senior commitment is evident from the announcement and given the likelihood that regular updates will be available on the organization's intranet. Consider a Kickoff meeting as optional. Conduct one if you think it will help convey the commitment and seriousness of the effort and provide an effective forum to answer questions. Skip it if it will just take up a large amount of time and everyone is likely to just react with "Yeah, we get it already." If you do include it, make sure it is integrated with the decision paper communications plan.

- <u>Don't Wait</u>. Be wary of waiting too long to get started. It is reasonable to make sure appropriate direction and resources are provided so that the DPAH team can productively begin its work. This is a warning not to *wait* for things that will properly be discovered and/or concluded during the course of the decision paper development. This type of waiting can be a political trap to interminably delay the decision paper development work. Embrace the process of discovery when developing a decision paper. Many of the things that make it into the final report will not be known at the start of the process.

Enough introduction; let's get started.

PART 1
The Standard Decision Paper Structure

A Standard Structure Helps Tell the Story

To maintain a good level of clarity, integrity, and completeness of your decision paper, you should follow a structure that ensures a logical flow of information. The structure will allow your "story" to build. I use the word *story* here and throughout the rest of the guide to emphasize that you are indeed writing a story in that it has a beginning, a middle, and an end. Once your readers begin to read it, they will want to continue to read it until it gets to the end. Your story will draw them in. It will be easy to understand. It will make sense. There will be no dead ends or confusing distractions.

Table 1. Standard Decision Paper Structure

	Section	Description
0.	Title	Easy to understand, positive in tone, outcome-oriented.
1.	Document Purpose	What this paper is intended to accomplish—its reason for being.
2.	Intended Audience	Who this document is written for, and its use restrictions.
3.	Background	All relevant historical information for the scope of the decision paper.
4.	The Need	Why a decision paper process is necessary in this situation.
5.	Scope	What to consider in the course of preparing the paper ("means") and in the final outputs ("ends") achieved by executing the recommendations.

	Section	Description
6.	Objectives	What we plan to accomplish, and to what priority. Business and system objectives focus on expected outcomes; Initiative Objectives (also called project objectives) focus on the work that will be conducted to meet the business and system objectives.
7.	Methodology	How we prepared the decision paper (means) and how we plan to accomplish the recommendations (ends): methods, techniques, practices, and manual and automated tools.
8.	Constraints, Assumptions and Dependencies	The hard limitations (constraints), reasonable givens (assumptions), and necessary prerequisites (dependencies).
9.	Issues	Items that are *at issue.* These must be resolved in order to achieve the objectives of the decision paper.
10.	Risks	Potential events that may impede or prevent the attainment of the decision paper's stated objectives.
11.	Findings	Relevant facts and evidence discovered are presented for consideration. (Analysis happens in the next section.)
12.	Analysis	Analysis of what the findings mean.
13.	Conclusions	The bold and creative step of drawing conclusions directly relevant to the scope and objectives of the decision paper.
14.	Alternatives and Recommendation	Reasonable and actionable alternatives—ways forward to achieve the scope and objectives—are presented. One alternative is offered as the recommendation.

	Section	Description
15.	Wrap-up	Summarize by cross-referencing scope and objectives to the actual work conducted and the alternatives and recommendations.

0. Title

The title is the first thing people will notice about your decision paper. It answers the question, "Tell me very quickly: what is this?" Like it or not, your readers will form an opinion as to its contents and value based on just a few words on the cover page. The title may draw them in, make them disinterested, repulse them, or actually make them angry. When handed the decision paper or when receiving it in an email, they may be required to read it, but whether they read it eagerly or reluctantly initially depends a good deal on the title.

There is no arguing the need for a title to a decision paper. The question is what it should be and what principles you should follow to come up with a title. Do not take this task lightly. A gripping title is essential for a successful decision paper. In just a few words, you must capture the scope and outcome of the paper.

Here are some suggestions on how to go about creating your title.

First, the "Do's" of Selecting a Title

- Be Positive. Unless there is an obvious circumstance that indicates otherwise, titles should be solution-oriented, not problem-oriented. Titles should look forward, not backward. For example, the title "Documenting the Failure of the Financial Systems Project" is not as effective as "Learning from the Failed Financial Systems Project." We do not obfuscate that the project failed; we just give it a more progressive title. The title "The Rivertown Plant Explosion Disaster" is accurate but negative; "Improving Safety—Learnings from the Rivertown Plant Explosion" is not just positive, it lets the reader have an inkling as to why he/she would want to read it. The first title might have a reader thinking the paper dwells on the negative without looking for practical learnings.

  In one quick fragment sentence, your title should optimistically project the future when considering an as yet unarticulated problem or opportunity.

- Focus on the End State, Not the Journey. Titles should suggest the outcome of the paper, not dwell on how you got there. For example, "Planning Steps to Close the Seattle Office" is much weaker than "Improving Our Business—Learnings from the Seattle Office Closing."

- <u>Focus on the Business End State, Not the Technical End State</u>. This is a problem I often see. We pay such overwhelming attention to the technical end state that we lose the business focus of the decision paper. For example, "Recommendations to Improve Factory Safe Operations" is a much more effective title than "Recommended Changes to Policy XY-003 Site Management."

- <u>Be Brief</u>. Titles should be short. Often, when you see an overly long title, this is a sign the author missed the point of the title. The title is not there to summarize the paper. It is not an abstract. It is a handle, an access point. The title should say enough to identify the scope and outcome of the decision paper at its very highest level. I am not in favor of providing guidance such as "A title should be x words or letters long." The topics of decision papers are too broad and varied for such advice. Use your judgment.

- <u>Noun, Verb or Sentence</u>. Your title is usually a thing rather than an action. It is usually not a complete sentence because that would make it overly long. Most often that means your title most resembles a noun or, more formally, a complex object or object clause.

- <u>Title Matches the Tenor</u>. Your title must match the tenor or theme of the decision paper. Decision papers that work in an arena of high risk and high gain should have a title that captures that tone. For example, the decision paper for the Strategy to Close the Lollipop Division that proposes to shut down the business line for which the company's brand is most well known should not be titled "Product Line Refocusing." "Strategic Product Realignment" might be okay, but it's still a little weak. "Strategies to Close Lollipop Division—Respecting a 100-Year-Old Product Line" might be better. Conversely, a decision paper that works in a tactical arena and has incremental recommendations should not have a title that seems to promise a large-scale change. So "Closing the Lollipop Division—Can Our Company Survive?" would not be a good title.

- <u>Titles from the Big Boss</u>. Title the decision paper according to the current understanding of the entire scope of the paper, regardless of what the big bosses are calling it. Executive management has a challenging task of staying abreast of the goings-on in an entire company or organization. When important situations arise, they may begin to use a convenient tag line to describe a problem. This is sometimes a result of very appropriate incident response processes. When an important issue arises, corporate incident response processes may require a briefing for the Board of Directors, the CEO, or other executives. As the problem evolves, more becomes known about the root cause. The original tag line can end up being misleading or simply completely inaccurate. For example, for the Failed Financial Systems Project, what started out as strong suspicions of software vendor product quality issues was later learned to be mostly caused by poor management of employees assigned to the project. Therefore, it would be inappropriate to give the decision paper a title based on the big bosses' initial impression, such as "Financial Systems Project—Getting Software Vendor Management Right."

Second, Some Cautions When Selecting a Title

- <u>Acronyms, Abbreviations and Jargon</u>. Be very wary of using acronyms, abbreviations, and jargon in a title. Such a practice may indeed keep the title short, but you may risk alienating all readers who don't have enough background in the subject of the paper to already know what these shortcuts or your particular argot means. If you must use acronyms and abbreviations, use ones that every reader could be reasonably expected to understand. For example, you will need to determine if everyone in your organization knows that the Strategy and Planning team is called SNP if you want to title the paper "Closing the Lollipop Division and Improving SNP Policy and Practice."

  Jargon is basically words some understand and others do not. Given that definition, I recommend that you never use jargon.

- <u>Beware of Negative Trigger Words</u>. Some words carry so much baggage that they would best be kept out of the title entirely. If an organization just experienced a $50 million failed project with an outsourcing company, be aware that you might immediately lose large portions of your audience if you put the word *outsourcing* in your decision paper title. For another example, I once worked at a bank where the CEO and CFO were overly (in my opinion) sensitive to hearing about projects or expenditures required for regulatory compliance purposes. Whenever they heard this—even when it was entirely logical and valid—anyone within earshot would have to listen to a long lecture about how we have to stop kowtowing to the regulators and that the regulators are not on equal footing with the shareholders, etc. etc. As a result, the executives or senior managers knew to never use the words *regulatory*, *compliance*, or *legal* in a project or decision paper title. We avoided that even when it would have made a lot of logical sense. Become familiar with the negative trigger words in your environment and stay away from them or use them with extreme caution.

Third, the "Don'ts" of Selecting a Title

- <u>Don't Be Funny</u>. It is never a good idea to inject humor into your decision paper title. When dealing with the type of serious topics decision papers deal with, humor cheapens and distracts. It makes the reader wonder if you are serious about this situation or just having a good time with it. These are not the types of impressions we want to leave.

  We have all noticed how news items (in print and electronic media) have fallen in love with cute, humorous titles for news and feature stories. Do not mimic this practice. The decision paper on closing the Lollipop Division should not have a cute title like "We're Licked—Closing the Lollipop Division." As well, the decision paper on the Seattle Office Closing should not be called "Seattle Skedaddle." These are funny where humor is not called for.

- <u>Avoid Tired Expressions</u>. Where possible, avoid hackneyed expressions, meaning expressions that are trite and overused. For one, they can sap the energy right out of your paper by making it sound like every other document the reader has seen. They also risk diluting what you want to communicate. For example, calling the paper "Paradigm Shift—Rethinking the Lollipop Division" leans on the tired, now almost meaningless term *paradigm shift.*

- Don't Be Generic. Don't select a title that could be used for any number of decision papers on any number of topics. "Recommendations from the Committee," "Product Enhancement," and "Service Line Report" are examples of titles that miss an opportunity to let the reader know a little bit about what the paper is actually about.

- Don't Model on Book Titles. Book titles (fiction or factual) are not good models for decision paper titles. Decision papers exist in a business or organizational context where reading the paper is required, so the title must capture the essence of the content. Really great works of fiction often have titles that require readers to immerse themselves into the book before really understanding how it relates to the content of the book. The title *Gone with the Wind* doesn't help you understand the story is about the U.S. Civil War, slavery, riches gained and then lost, love and conflict, etc.; you have to start reading the book to make the connection. If you wrote a decision paper with a similarly cryptic title, few people would go out of their way to read it.

- Don't Obfuscate. When creating a title, be sure to avoid obfuscating the real situation. Typically this is done for the sake of avoiding blaming those who may indeed be the source of much of the trouble that led to the decision paper in the first place. The Rivertown Plant Explosion was a serious event, with lives lost. Don't obfuscate that seriousness with a weak title such as "Rivertown Plant Safety" or, worse, "Rivertown Plant—Unforeseen Safety Event." While parties who are concerned about their own culpability in this event may find comfort in the word *unforeseen* making its way into the decision paper title, it is wrong to exonerate anyone in the title.

- Caution on Subtitles. I recommend not using lengthy subtitles for a decision paper. They are a distraction from the title. Whatever calcifications or additional thoughts a long subtitle may provide can better be provided in the body of the document.

Summary

Choose titles carefully. Make them easy to understand, positive in tone, and more outcome-oriented than process-oriented. Short titles are good, but don't sacrifice clarity and completeness for brevity.

1. Document Purpose

How to Write the Document Purpose Section

The Document Purpose section is usually very brief—a paragraph or two. It describes the decision paper's reason for being. It answers the question "What is this decision paper for?" If you were to leave this short section out, you would risk your readers beginning to work through the paper while constantly asking themselves, "What is this all about, anyway? Where are the authors going with this?" If you were to leave it out, detractors (including those who may have political or selfish reasons to dispute the logic of the paper) would have an opportunity to redefine the purpose of your decision paper and pronounce it a failure.

The Document Purpose allows you to make the scope and objectives of the paper clear right at the beginning. One should be able to read the title and the Document Purpose section and know what the document is about and why it exists.

The reasons for writing a decision paper vary. Whatever they are, you will need to summarize them briefly in the Document Purpose. Here are some common types of decision paper Document Purposes:

- Business Case. These decision papers lay out a logical argument to act, decide, and/or invest based on a need or opportunity, and considerations of cost, benefit, and risk.

- Project Business Case. These decision papers are a special kind of business case decision paper in which a project will be initiated should the business case be approved.

- Investigation. These decision papers analyze a problem or situation and recommend action. Typical incidents include disasters, failures, cybersecurity breaches, and suspected crimes or malfeasance. Be careful when using the term *investigation* because, in some corporate cultures, it is a trigger word that may be interpreted negatively.

- Checkpoint or Milestone. Some decision papers are written as part of a process to monitor, analyze, and report on a business process, launch, or project as it is underway. There is no special trigger, such as a problem; only the reaching of a certain point on a plan or calendar that results in the initiation of such a decision paper.

- Exploration. These decision papers weigh the positives and negatives of an opportunity. That means there is no "problem" or "issue" to solve, just a situation or investment that may be favorably exploited.

- Compliance Responsibility. These decision papers are written to fulfill a legal or regulatory requirement to document an event or recommend an action. Often an aspect of their reason for being is to develop the appropriate responses to laws and regulations where the exact response required is ambiguous.

- Lessons Learned. These decision papers examine a situation (often a problematic one), document Lessons Learned, and recommend systemic changes in process, technology, organization, etc. In some organizational cultures (such as in some branches of the military), these are called After Action Reviews. They are typically written after the problematic situation has been resolved and there has been a period of stability with no new related issues.

- Issue Resolution. Sometimes decision papers are written to resolve an issue, which is to say they are written to resolve a conflict between decision makers, determine a course of action where more than one course of action is available, or determine a course of action when some believe there is no way to reach a successful outcome.

The Document Purpose is end-state oriented. By that I mean it focuses on the outcomes that will result from following the recommendations in the decision paper. So, for example, the Document Purpose for the Strategy to Close the Lollipop Division decision paper will state that the purpose of the decision paper is to develop a comprehensive and actionable plan that will wind down the Lollipop Division. The plan will explicitly consider the approach to informing and working in partnership with customers, suppliers, grocery chains, labor unions, news media, and local municipal governments in the areas where lollipop production will be discontinued. To continue with this example, the Document Purpose is *not* to plan and conduct several site visits to plants, customers, and governments to research the best approaches to the wind-down. That will indeed be done, but it is a *means*, not an *end*.

Here are some suggestions on how to go about creating an effective Document Purpose:

- <u>Simple Start</u>. I recommend starting the Document Purpose with the words *The purpose of this document is*. This is clear, simple and to the point. There's no need to make the reader sift through preliminary words when what they really want to know is why this document was written.

- <u>Common Language</u>. The Document Purpose must be understandable to anyone, even those with absolutely no background in or knowledge of what the paper is about. Consider that it may be read by new employees, outside auditors, etc. Some industry-specific terminology may be necessary in the rest of the decision paper's content, but the Document Purpose section must be easy for anyone to understand. In this respect, it resembles a newspaper or magazine article on a scientific topic. The reader of the *New York Times* newspaper is not expected to be a physicist, so a NYT article about the Large Hadron Collider in Geneva will be written in a way most people can read and understand.

- <u>Formal Document</u>. Some decision papers, such as business cases, after action reports, and product innovation analyses, are formally required in an organization. If (and only if) that is the case in your organization, it is okay and probably a good idea to state that in the Document Purpose. For example, in a Lessons Learned paper for the Failed Financial Systems Project, the Document Purpose might say: "This document is a formal Post Project Review of the Financial Systems Project. The board-approved project management policy mandates a Post Project Review for all projects of $5 million of capital or more."

- <u>Limit to the Purpose of the Document</u>. For reasons that I do not fully understand, whenever I ask someone to include a Document Purpose in a decision paper, they usually include a broad range of other topics in this little section as well. Somehow the author feels compelled to have language on benefits, risks, alternatives, etc. in this section. It might be that the authors do not feel like they are doing a thorough enough job when limited to a paragraph or two. Or maybe they are so eager to get on with the substance of the paper or are so enamored with the content that they have to add it where it does not belong. Don't add extra content to the Document Purpose section.

- It is Document Purpose, not Project Purpose. This section is there to inform the reader on why the *document* exists. If the decision paper is examining a project, initiative, or business line, or proposing a new project or other new endeavor, that content is discussed elsewhere in the paper. Limit the language in this section to the purpose of the document.

- Findings and Recommendations Come Later. Some writers, whom I would consider overzealous, pepper their paper with statements indicating that they think the outcome of the paper is so obvious that it needs to be mentioned where it does not belong—such as in the Document Purpose. For example, the authors of the Seattle Office Closing decision paper may believe (and feel) that it is obvious that the company should not let a new office operate at a net financial loss and that those behind the opening of the Seattle office should be punished. They would, incorrectly, have their Document Purpose say, "The purpose of this document is to make clear that there are repercussions for violating the policy that operating units must contribute to net margin, without exception." It would be better to say, "The purpose of this document is to review the decision to close the Seattle office and to recommend practical Lessons Learned in areas of organization, policy, strategy planning and operations."

- Stay True to the Mission. Decision papers are typically commissioned with the genuine intention that the author conducts research and analysis to a level of depth not conducted before. As such, the Document Purpose, staying true to its mission, would not imply the conclusion that is being reached in the paper (if one skips ahead to the Recommendation section). Instead, the Document Purpose defines the outcome scope.

Political Misapplications

Those misrepresenting the Document Purpose may have a less than admirable agenda of their own to push. It will be important to use and re-use the Document Purpose language throughout the entire decision paper. You would not want, for example, those with a strong resistance to change to succeed in convincing others the purpose of the decision paper for the Strategies to Close the Lollipop Division is to "justify and whitewash the mismanagement of one of the company's most important product lines." While you cannot control what bad actors say, using the language of the Document Purpose consistently throughout the document makes it more likely that those who hear their misrepresentations will immediately recognize them as false.

Summary

The Document Purpose is very short and allows the reader to understand, up front, what the decision paper is intended to accomplish—its reason for being. It excludes the rest of the story that unfolds in the decision paper. That is what the remaining sections are for.

2. Intended Audience

How to Write the Intended Audience Section

This section is optional. If it is clear who the Intended Audience is after reading the Document Purpose, or if the Intended Audience is a broad range of people and organizations, there is no need for an Intended Audience section.

However, if the Intended Audience is restricted and/or targeted, this section is an important, albeit brief, requirement.

Here are some suggestions on how to go about creating an effective Intended Audience section:

- Clear and Brief. I recommend you begin the Intended Audience section with the words *This decision paper, [Title], is intended to be read by.*

- Actual Department Names. When stating the Intended Audience, you will need to refer to parts of an organization (i.e., departments, divisions, teams, etc.). Use actual organization names and not local vernacular for the name. If a department is often called "F&A" or "Finance" but its actual name is Finance, Accounting and Treasury, then use the actual name.

- Titles, Not Names. Similar to the recommendation on departments, use titles rather than the names of persons when the Intended Audience is narrowly targeted to just a few individuals. If Bill Jones is the VP of Corporate Compliance today, there is no guarantee he will be in that role tomorrow. If, in this example, the Intended Audience includes this position, then state the position's exact title and leave the name of the person currently occupying that position out.

As you define the Intended Audience in this section, do not lose sight of what we described in the introduction: your decision paper will be read by a broad range of people, including those with little to no prior knowledge of the subject of the paper. That means even though you are giving good thought to your Intended Audience, you still must produce an entire decision paper that can be read and understood by *anyone*.

Secret or Confidential

Some decision papers are confidential and/or secret. Whether the reasons for the secrecy are legal or political does not matter much to the decision paper author. But, as the author, you must determine whether the paper should indeed be limited to only a select few readers for such reasons. In this situation, you will include, where appropriate, imperative language that those outside of certain groups should not read the paper. If the reader is in such a proscribed group and is in the process of reading the paper, the Intended Audience section should tell them to put it aside and take specific actions as required.

Usage Restrictions

Where warranted, it may be advisable to call this section "Intended Audience and Usage Restrictions." This way you can use this section to both limit the readership and also direct the readers on what they may or may not do with the information they glean from the paper. This is a special circumstance that would be explained to the authors when the decision paper is commissioned. A common restriction is that no one may forward the working drafts and final decision paper report to anyone else. Such requests should be directed to the Decision Paper Ad Hoc team leaders. This will allow a measure of control over the distribution. For example, when the DPAH team knows exactly who is reviewing the drafts, it can then ensure that every reviewer receives updates.

Recourse to Expand Audience

You may include some language as to what process the reader may follow if they would like the paper distributed outside of its Intended Audience.

Political Misapplications

You will find in less mature or less healthy organizational cultures that restrictions in the Intended Audience section may become fodder for conspiracy theorists. There are many legitimate reasons to limit the distribution of a decision paper. Even if it is not confidential, it helps to limit the distribution so that parts of the company do not get distracted by work that is already being taken care of. Yet I have seen cases where someone portrays an innocent and forthright restriction for the sake of efficiency as an attempt on the part of the authors to "suppress" the document.

A good way to deal with these types of political games is to get very clear direction and validation from the decision paper governance structure as to the need for restrictions on distribution. Recall my advice in the introduction to get governance at the highest level possible. This is one reason for that. Obtain explicit, very senior-level review and approval of the contents of the Intended Audience section. It will then be harder for those with bad political motives to criticize any audience restrictions.

Summary

The Intended Audience section is an optional section that lets the reader know who the document is written for and, if applicable, the restrictions on the sharing and use of its information. It may also be called "Intended Audience and Usage Restrictions."

3. Background

How to Write the Background Section

The Background section describes historical events and circumstances that are relevant, sometimes directly and sometimes indirectly, to the purpose (i.e., Document Purpose) of the decision paper. Background sections also give the decision paper a context so that the reader can better understand what led to a commitment to devote time, energy, and money to a decision paper analysis. In the art of developing excellent decision papers, good Background sections are essential. They are the equivalent of getting a common understanding before engaging in discovery, deep thought, analysis, and debate.

In my experience, the Background section is one of those most misunderstood by decision paper authors and, not coincidentally, often poorly executed. I advise including a Background section as a way to make the whole decision paper easier to understand. Ultimately, the recommendations in the decision paper will make sense only in a historical and environmental context. Authors often write their first drafts without a Background section only to add one later when initial readers get confused about what historical events led to the need for a decision paper.

Here are some suggestions on how to go about creating an effective Background section:

- Chronological. Most often, it is useful to write the Background section so that it progresses through relevant history chronologically. The alternative is hopscotching through history based on some other structure. This can be very confusing.

- Big Event. The only exception to the preceding guideline is when there has been a big event that is likely top of mind to your readers. For example, if this paper is being written to recommend improvements in safety after the Rivertown Plant explosion that killed several factory employees, it would be wise to begin the Background section with an acknowledgement that this is the most important part of the Background. Once that is accomplished, then the author can describe the events chronologically, including the big event wherever it occurred in history.

- <u>Dates</u>. If you have exact dates when events took place, by all means use them. That the decision by the Executive Committee to approve the new Seattle office took place on an exact date is interesting and relevant. Include the date.

- <u>Relevant History</u>. The entire point of the Background section is to inform the reader of relevant history. When you do this, make sure to include details of history that, while they may have no importance to the purpose and substance of the decision paper, are nonetheless necessary to help the reader understand other parts of the Background that are relevant.

- <u>Factual</u>. Background sections should hew as closely as humanly possible to the facts. Therefore, be very careful to avoid interpretation or words that ascribe motive. For example, if the prior Financial Systems project failed because the system requirements used in product selection were incomplete, then say just that. Be very careful about writing things such as "the team was careless in its attention to detail" or "the team was rushed, by an artificial deadline from senior management, to publish the requirements before they were ready." Generally, such motive or root cause is impossible to know and/or is debatable. When it is impossible to know, leave it out.

  Be mindful of the importance of sticking to the facts as you write and revise your Background section. It is a difficult guideline to follow. Just to give you a little more help with this, consider that the sentence "The explosion that killed 6 employees was likely caused by small fissure-like cracks in the engine block." is more factual than "The explosion that killed 6 employees was likely caused by small fissure-like cracks in the engine that were noticed but ignored by the safety inspectors on site." In the Background section, the basic rule of thumb is to document what is factual or observable and stay away from root causes that would require the author to either have the supernatural ability to peer into people's souls to understand their thoughts and motivations or do further analysis of the sort that will be revealed in the decision paper sections on Findings and Analysis.

- <u>Prior Investigations</u>. One exception to the preceding guideline is not really an exception at all. It is okay to ascribe motive or opine on root causes when a prior investigation, report, or analysis documented a conclusion as to such motives and causes. In this case, be careful to cite the source and state that the source report stated that this was the cause. In our plant explosion example, it is okay to say "Regarding the similar accident event 9 years ago, an independent investigation conducted by the State University Engineering Department reached the conclusion that the on-site safety inspectors must have known of the flaws but ignored them." The reason this is not an exception to the factual guideline even though it departs from fact to motive is that the fact that is being presented is what the report stated, not that what the report stated is true. It might even help to state immediately after that sentence, "This conclusion has not been substantiated or refuted by any other analysis or report." Now you are merely stating factual background and not taking positions about motives.

- Disputed Facts. Where facts are in dispute, then Background sections may present sets of facts and merely comment that there are differing perspectives on what actually happened. If these differing perspectives were presented with emotion and vitriol, just leave out the emotion and vitriol and state the viewpoints. In our explosion example, merely state that "Regarding a similar event nine years ago, the Safety Inspectors Union Leader, Joe Smith, issued a statement at the time denying that the cause was attributable to the inspectors and instead questioned the quality of the foreign-made safety valves that were recently installed. The State University engineering review did not find safety or quality issues with the valves." Whether the university professors or union leaders said nasty things to each other or shared their views in an atmosphere of mutual respect or mutual animosity is not important to this Background section. Leave that type of analysis to others (such as senior management or Human Resources) since this decision paper is heading toward a recommendation on safety improvements. Those emotions are not relevant to that mission. What is relevant is that a somewhat similar accident happened nine years ago, and it is useful to summarize that history in the Background section.

- Stick to History. For reasons I do not fully understand, decision paper authors often will place in the Background section information that belongs in a Findings, Analysis, Conclusions, or Recommendation section. Avoid this pitfall and stick to history.

For example, in the Seattle Office Closing decision paper, it would be wrong to include the following in the Background section: "As will be shown later in this paper, the financial models the Corporate Strategy team used to project income and revenue growth were very deficient, omitting key expenditures from the net income projections." For the sake of the example, let's say that statement is true. It still does not belong in the Background section. Better for a Background section would be "The executive team relied on financial models estimating revenue and net income, as produced by the Corporate Strategy team and presented at the May 20xx Executive Leadership Team meeting." Notice how some might argue about the first phrasing—they could disagree that key expenditures were omitted or that they were material—but one cannot argue with the second wording. The decision paper is structured so that the story of findings, analyses, conclusions, and recommendations will be told in due course. Allow that story to unfold.

- Common Ground. One objective of a well-written Background section is that all readers will finish reading the Background and have no argument with its content. The Background section then establishes a baseline of history on which all readers, regardless of their perspective, can agree. This *common ground* is essential to a decision paper so that the paper can build on the factual basis of the Background before going into other, perhaps more disputable or controversial sections. For example, a decision paper that supports the management decision to close the Seattle office, even though it has only been open for 24 months, might have a Background section that notes, "The original business case for the new Seattle office was approved by the Executive Committee with all parties voting for the new office except for the representative from Marketing, who voted against." This doesn't say the Marketing representative was right all along. It doesn't say the Marketing representative was smarter than everyone else, thought the selected Seattle site was in the wrong part of town, or had a better understanding of the financials in the business case. It just says the inarguable fact that the meeting minutes show the vote, and the vote is transcribed into this Background—with no commentary or editorializing.

- <u>Name Names</u>. Unlike the Intended Audience section, in the Background section, it is important to name names when such facts are available so that the background presented is factual. If CEO Mary Jones approved the Seattle Office Business Case, then say that. There is no need to obscure who actually made this final decision. It is needlessly confusing to instead say the Seattle Office Business Case was approved "at the highest levels" or "by the CEO at the time." Did you notice how gnawingly annoying those last two examples would be if you were reading this decision paper with a keen interest in knowing the factual history? Clearly the author could have told you who made the decision but just left if out. I can see the annoyed reader writing in the margin: "Find out if this was Jones or Bronson. Not sure?"

- <u>Include All That is Relevant</u>. Good Background sections include all that is relevant, regardless of anything else. This means including facts from within the organization and outside the organization. It means including things that may have been annoying or disagreeable. It means including things that seemed consequential at the time but proved to be irrelevant in the final analysis. In our example of the decision paper recommending improvements in response to a fatal plant explosion, it may be relevant to note the government's safety regulations in place at the time of the accident. And include the company's adherence (or not) to these regulations to the extent that is known. That you later concluded that this had no bearing on the accident or aftermath is not important in the Background. Cover that later in the paper.

- <u>Reread and Rewrite</u>. Once you have drafted the decision paper completely, you will need to reread and likely rewrite the Background section. The reason is that the process of logically stepping through the decision paper, as you have done in writing it, will reveal gaps in the Background. A finding, for example, that the Seattle office site ultimately selected was not one of the final three locations presented to the Executive Committee as possible alternatives means that the Background section should include a summary of the policy and practices for new site selection and the standard roles of the Facilities Department and the Executive Committee in that process. In this example, any finding or recommendation in the area of the site selection process will require readers to understand the baseline process in place before they can reasonably be expected to support any recommendations to change the process and/or improve enforcement of the existing process.

- Historical Unknowns. Some things in the Background will be both relevant and unknown. It will be important to delineate what is known and what is unknown without much speculation regarding the unknowns. Was the machinery that ultimately exploded mishandled in shipping on its way to the factory? The manufacturer may have speculated that that was a root cause. However, no one around knows anything about it. All that can be said in the Background is that the manufacturer has speculated (and gone as far as to document that speculation) that the machinery was damaged en route to the factory but that this can neither be confirmed nor disproved.

- Very Bad Facts. Some facts represent, subjectively speaking, very bad or unpleasant news. In our Seattle office decision paper, perhaps there was an email discovered from the Northwest Regional VP to one of his Senior Relationship Managers that said he would ignore the site selection of the Executive Leadership Committee because he felt they were (to quote the email) "a bunch of idiots," and perhaps the email went on to describe how the VP selected a different site. When writing a decision paper, it is important to merely state the facts, despite how objectively awful they may appear, in plain language without any embellishment. So our decision paper Background might read, in part: "During the post-project review conducted by the Project Office, an email was discovered and authenticated that indicated Bill Johnson, Northwest Regional VP, knew that he was selecting a site that was not approved by the Executive Committee and decided to commit to an alternative site without further consultation with company management."

- Very Good Facts. Some facts represent, subjectively speaking, excellent news that may be inspiring and wonderful. In our plant machinery explosion example, the Head Foreman manually activated the fire suppression systems, at great danger to herself, when these systems failed to activate automatically. Firefighters on site later documented that this act saved many lives. In this case, as with the very bad news, just state the facts. Avoid sappy statements about how we are all greatly indebted to Foreman Cheryl Knolls for her brave and selfless actions. Such language may have much relevance at company meetings, in press releases, etc., but it does not belong in a decision paper. Merely state: "Firefighters who responded to the scene documented that the explosion could very well have caused more fatalities and more damage were it not for the fact that Foreman Cheryl Knolls manually activated the fire suppression systems when they failed to activate automatically." No sap. Just the facts.

- <u>Don't Judge</u>. Do not judge; do not interpret. Even though the Northwest Regional VP broke several rules in HR and IT Acceptable Use policies when he wrote his email calling fellow employees "idiots," do not judge. Just state that the content of the emails was deemed to be outside of HR's Respect in the Workplace policy when reviewed by the Head of HR.

- <u>Irrelevant Facts</u>. As the author of the decision paper, you have the advantage of knowing what historical facts are relevant to the findings and recommendations in the report and what are not. Frequently, there are "red herrings" in the plots of decision papers. By this I mean there are facts that seem to be relevant but turn out to be extraneous, and perhaps, in the author's view, they are completely meaningless and irrelevant. Generally, you must include these facts in your Background section irrespective of their ultimate relevance. You include them because your readers are not there yet—as they read the Background section, they have not yet followed the logical path you will be taking them through. If you leave out items they think are relevant, they will just be disturbed about the exclusion. They might even accuse you, the author, of ignoring important details. The omitted facts may not have played any role. But your readers will consider it relevant and may be wondering about it, so it is best to include it. For example, if the brand of safety helmets in use changed right before the plant accident, you are best advised to mention that in the Background. If later you determined that this was not meaningful in any way to the accident, injuries, or fatalities, then say that in the Findings section.

- <u>Highly Technical Details</u>. Sometimes a highly technical detail is relevant to the Background. If, for example, in the Failed Financial Systems Project, there was a situation where the Lead Technical Architect lost an argument with Central Procurement to purchase servers with dual RAID processors and this appeared to contribute to the system problems later, then you must give a high-level layman's view of what dual RAID processors are and what they do. In part, it could read like this: "During the Architecture stage of the project, the Lead Technical Architect specified servers be ordered that made use of 'dual RAID processors.' Procurement did not follow this specification and instead purchased servers with directly attached storage. The servers purchased by Procurement were $30K each, while the servers with dual RAID processors were $50K each. Without going into technical details, the dual RAID processor servers are designed to recover from hardware failures without the applications (including the Financial Systems) going down. The servers without the dual RAID processors are more likely to fail, with such failures causing outages and disruptions to the Finance Department users."

- <u>Questions in the Reader's Mind</u>. A good Background section answers questions that are already active in the reader's mind. Consider how a reader would be very interested to know if all machinery at other factories of the same type as the one that exploded at Rivertown were inspected and determined to not be of potential harm to the employees who handle them. Consider how they would want to know what happened to these other machines and whether they are, right now, endangering other employees' lives. You must put yourself in the position of the reader and come up with the natural questions they would have about the history and current state of the situation, and then answer them in the Background.

- <u>Why</u>. In the Background section, you usually don't know enough to address "why" questions. So don't try to. That is why the decision paper is being written in the first place.

  "Why" is the most interesting of the list of questions (who, what, where, when, how, why) people have about anything. Why did the Northwest Regional VP select a Seattle office site not approved by executive management? Why did the machinery explode? Why was the financial system so riddled with errors and problems when it was supposed to be close to readiness for implementation? Why couldn't we create ingenious marketing ideas to sustain and grow the lollipop business? These are good questions. They are not answered in the Background section. They are likely answered in the totality of the decision paper.

- Length Doesn't Matter. Background sections may be short or long. There is no single right length for a Background section. Avoid shortening a Background section merely for the sake of having a short section.

Political Misapplications

Those misrepresenting the decision paper Background section may have a less than admirable agenda of their own to push. Such bad political actors may take a few approaches to undermine the credibility of the Background section:

- Dispute Facts. While it sounds odd, I have often seen those with less than pure agendas just flat-out argue with facts. If this is happening, the most effective approach I have found to deal with it is to give the accusers the floor at a formal meeting so that they can express their views. Let them dispute the facts. For example, the Background section in the Failed Financial Systems Project decision paper may note that all appropriate policies, processes, check points and approvals were followed when selecting the software vendor. This is not consistent with a rumor that the IT Project Manager decided on the vendor on his own, without any consultation. If such a rumor is flat-out false, then do not give in; do not change the Background section to include this false accusation. Just invite the accusers and the IT Project Manager (the accused) to a meeting to discuss.

- Asking for Interpretation. Some reviewers of a Background section will not understand that the section is purely for background material. They will argue for the inclusion of what we would call analyses and recommendations. For example, why can't we just say the VP of Product Strategy is incompetent, since the company finds itself with no choice but to shut down or sell the Lollipop Division? Whether a senior manager or a company function did not do their work adequately is a topic for the Analysis section. The Background section may just list some facts such as: "Sales in the Lollipop Division as issued annually by the Product Strategy team did not meet targets for each of the current and prior six years."

- Selective Criticism. I will draw an example from US politics. Approximately 15 years ago, a prominent Republican senator and a prominent Democratic governor (in separate events) were caught paying for and using prostitutes for sex. Both were married, and both were exposed and shamed in the press. Those monitoring the commentary of other office holders and political leaders would have noticed condemnation was louder from the Republicans criticizing the Democratic governor, and from the Democrats criticizing the Republican senator. There was almost no intra-party criticism. And so it will often go with criticism of decision paper Background sections. Those with impure motives will look to remove facts that indicate failings in their own organizations. DPAH leadership and team members should simply just resist this tactic.

Regardless of what tactic bad political actors use to undermine the Background section, the best defense is to keep the Background section thorough, purely background, and factual—without interpretation or editorializing.

Summary

The Background section contains all relevant and related historical information for the scope of the decision paper. By the time the reader has read and absorbed the entire Background section:

- The reader is clear as to why the decision paper was written. Together, the Document Purpose and Background sections have accomplished this.

- All the reader's questions about the history of the matter have been answered.

- The reader is ready and eager to move on.

- The reader, regardless of their own history with the subject matter of this decision paper, is very well prepared to understand the entire paper.

- Any gaps, misgivings, and suspicions the reader had about historical events are gone because they were addressed explicitly in the Background section.

4. The Need

How to Write the Need Section

'The Need' section describes the compelling requirement for this decision paper. In a way, it answers the questions, "Why don't we just skip developing this decision paper?' and "What possible good could come from this decision paper exercise?" The reason for the decision paper is that, in order to move forward, it is imperative that something be accomplished or thought through. Often, there is a problem that it would be irresponsible to ignore. Your section titled "The Need" describes why that is so. The Need section makes *the need* for the decision paper unambiguous.

There are a few principles to consider:

- Problem. The subject of the decision paper may be a problem, something that clearly went wrong or is problematic. The situation demands that some things be understood, the current problem remedied, and changes made so that this problem does not happen again. Decision papers that focus solely on solving a problem sometimes call the Need section a Problem Statement. In my experience, most decision papers are developed to solve a problem.

- Opportunity. The subject of the decision paper may be an opportunity for investigation, discovery, and learning something new, different, or original. Or it may be the opportunity to invest or initiate in areas with potential for gain or good. The Need section makes this clear. There may be great advantages to analyzing and learning, then recommending and acting. Note the lack of a problem to fix in the *opportunity* need.

- Mandate. Some decision papers are required as the result of a demand from an empowered source, such as the board of directors, senior executives, policy, law, or regulation (i.e., a compliance need). In those cases, it may be tempting to have a short "The Need" section that merely states the mandate. This is not good enough. You will *need* to get to the underlying reason or motivation for such a mandate. If the project policy demands a decision paper analysis of all projects that exceed their budgets by 100% or more, you will need to say that *and* explain why that is. The need is the "why," not simply the fact that such a mandate exists.

- Sustainment and/or Continuous Improvement. Some decision papers are required as a checkpoint to course-correct to keep a business line or functional area operating successfully—sustaining or improving their current levels of production. I would consider this as a special case of seizing an opportunity. One could envision, for example, at the same corporation that is ending its Lollipop Division, a decision paper may propose a thorough review of the Cupcake Division as a proactive, preventative step to make sure it does not die the slow and controversial demise experienced by the Lollipop Division.

Some ways our example scenarios may articulate The Need:

- Example—Failed Financial Systems Project. It is widely believed that excessive time and effort were expended with much disruption and interruption to other activities in the attempt to get the Financial Systems project to a successful conclusion with live systems, new features, and updated reporting. Despite this investment in time and dollars, the project was stopped; work effort and investments were wasted and written off. The enterprise *needs* to learn from any missteps that may have occurred in the project so that they do not happen again.

- Example—Rivertown Plant Explosion. Any plant safety event that results in death and serious injury to employees *needs* a thorough investigation and adoption of changes in practices, training, and technology so that such an event does not occur again.

- Example—Seattle Office Closing. The financial business case, including the target expansion in market presence and customer base, was not achieved from the creation and operation of the new Seattle office. The company *needs* to learn from this event so that it does not make the same mistake in the expansion and planning for other regions.

- Example—Strategies to Close the Lollipop Division. Now that it is clear that the Lollipop Division product line and business must be shut down and/or sold off, the business *needs* a clear strategy for accomplishing this—one that adequately deals with the constituencies and stakeholders, such as customers, employees, distributors, retailers, and regulators. There is also a need to learn from this very public and impactful product line closure, for the good of the company's other products.

Build on the Background

The Background section would have provided all relevant *background* data that supports the need for this decision paper. For example, the Background section could have shown the functions and capabilities that were not supported by the incumbent/legacy financial systems even though users viewed them as required. The Background section shows that information without any interpretation. The Need section can refer to that information, note that the gaps between functionality and perceived need were not filled, and draw a conclusion that this indicates a need to understand the root cause and remedy it for future projects.

Strategic Vision

Every organization should have a strategic vision. It is inspiring, long-term focused, and a concept everyone in the organization can relate to and rally around. This vision already exists; it is not created for the decision paper initiative. It is useful to consider whether the decision paper initiative supports the strategic vision. If so, include that in the Need section. Explain how it relates to and assists in achieving the organization's vision. It is not always the case, because some decision papers are firmly grounded in tactics and operations and do not do much to further the achievement of the organization's strategic vision.

Political Misapplications

Those misrepresenting the Need section may have their own less than admirable agenda to push. Bad political actors will argue either that there is no real need for the decision paper or that the need is of such low priority that the decision paper analysis should be deferred. The probability that those trying to undermine a decision paper exercise will do what they can to kill it is the Need section's primary reason for being. It is why this topic is not subsumed within another section, such as Document Purpose.

Be wary of those arguing that there is a need but that it is a low priority. Getting important activities deferred is a key tactic for those who ultimately want no action whatsoever. Continually diverting key resources, for example, is one way to continually defer a decision paper analysis. It is sneaky, but one can more easily get a decision paper deferred for, say, six months than get it cancelled. Meanwhile, the detractors have another six months to find another way to kill the paper, and the feeling of urgency has another six months to fade.

Summary

The Need section makes very clear why the analysis and recommendations of a decision paper process are necessary in this situation.

5. Scope

How to Write the Scope Section

The Scope section is often combined with the Objectives section into a "Scope and Objectives" section. I will leave that to you. For this guide, we separate them to make explaining their content clearer.

Scope is what constituent components the analysis will consider and will not consider, *and* what the end product will include and exclude. Note that it is important to define the scope of both the analysis (the means) and the end product (the ends).

In Scope

As described in the introduction of this guide, Means is the course of doing the work—that is, doing the work presented in the decision paper. Ends are the final product, the ultimate output, the result. The ends usually, if not always, come after the preparation and approval of the decision paper. The ends are created by the actions after the approval of the recommendations in the decision paper.

Usually, fully understanding the ends gives very few clues to what was done to reach those ends—the means. This concept will draw a clean distinction between the course of work to get something done and the final product. You must understand and internalize this, or your decision paper will make no sense. To completely convey your work, you need to provide detail on the scope of the means and the scope of the ends.

Table 2. Scope Examples

These examples are not exhaustive, just representative.

Decision Paper	Scope—Means	Scope—Ends
Failed Financial Systems Project	• Project team organization, reporting relationships, composition and competencies • Documents reviewed • Interviews conducted • Methodology followed / techniques employed • Metrics and data analyzed (including for the several testing phases)	• Recommendations for all aspects of project management and systems development—methods, tools, deliverables • Recommendations for project governance and controls • Recommendations for project metrics, go/no-go milestones, and reporting • Recommendations for revisions to key project roles, including Project Owner, Project Sponsor, Project Manager, Project Steering Committee
Rivertown Plant Explosion	• Safety and process policies and operational documents • Incident reports • Interviews of employees and contractors on site during and before the incident • First responders' reports	• Recommendations for changes in assembly and setup of machinery • Recommendations for frequency and content of safety checks • Recommendations for changes to safety and operational policies and processes

Decision Paper	Scope—Means	Scope—Ends
	• Machinery specs and procurement documentation	• Recommended Human Resources actions—suspend, dismiss, reprimand, etc.
Seattle Office Closing	• Interviews of local (Seattle) and head office managers involved in the decision to create and the processes to establish and support the Seattle office • Review of originally approved Seattle Office Business Case • Review of Seattle office performance reports, including revenue, income, customer satisfaction, new customer acquisition, and customer loyalty index	• Recommendations for changes to the strategy of creating satellite offices, including the possibility of ceasing this strategy • Recommendations for the annual customer, revenue, income, and net margin estimating process • Recommendations for changes to policy, process, and approval steps for new strategic ventures, including satellite offices • Clarification of reporting / responsibility relationships between satellite office managers and corporate function and product organizations
Strategies to Close the Lollipop Division	• Historical sales and profitability reporting analyzed • Customer and market sentiment analysis; net promoter score • Competitive analysis	• Strategy document describing approach and step-by-step schedule of activities for closing the Lollipop Division

Decision Paper	Scope—Means	Scope—Ends
	• Future projections of cost and availability analyzed • Grocery satisfaction surveys	

A very simple way to ensure you are capturing scope completely is to run through the 5 Ws and 1 H set of questions: Who, What, Where, When, Why, and How. Do this with thoughtful deliberation and rigor. It will provide you with confidence in the completeness of your Scope section. For example, who had a role in the lead-up, execution, and management of the idea to open a Seattle satellite office? Answering that question will help you see that the Financial Planning team in the Finance Department should be part of the means scope of the decision paper.

As you develop your decision paper and review drafts with key stakeholders, rights holders, and owners, you should be asking for close scrutiny of the Scope section. Most often you will get recommendations (or demands) to add to scope. Whether your scope needs to be added to will vary with each decision paper you develop. However, it will be important to finalize and get all involved on the same page as to scope. Your decision paper and its findings and recommendations could be argued to be worthless if you allow others to dismiss them because they say you left important constituent components out of the analysis and/or the end product.

I usually advise that it is better to add to scope than to take away. This flies in the face of the advice others may offer; many say scope should be *tight* and well controlled. To that I say, "Yes, but . . ." Yes, but in so doing, you will allow others to dismiss your work entirely on the basis that key work was not done and/or key outputs were not produced. A slightly larger scope to lessen the effectiveness of this tactic commonly employed by detractors is worth it, in my view.

Out of Scope

It is just as important to document what is out of scope as it is to document what is in scope. A key reason to make sure to clearly document what is not in scope is that it allows you to deal with the "you forgot" mindless accusations that may follow deliberate actions to put items out of scope. For example, a statement that "you forgot" to interview third-shift employees at the Rivertown plant is best dealt with proactively, with a note in the Scope section that only daytime shift employees will be interviewed and a clear explanation as to why this makes sense.

Political Misapplications

You will find in less mature or less healthy organizational cultures that the Scope section may be miscommunicated and weaponized. You may be accused of excluding items from Scope in order to cover up some aspects that should have been reviewed and analyzed. Some may accuse you of "stacking the deck" in favor of one conclusion or another by including areas in scope that will clearly be found to be problematic. The simple way to deal with this is to make sure the Scope, when in draft form, is reviewed by a wide audience of constituents, stakeholders, and rights holders. Getting the Scope section approved by the governance process *during* the preparation of the decision paper will be important to completing the Scope so that the *story* of the decision paper can proceed as later sections are developed.

Summary

The Scope section makes very clear what will be considered and evaluated in the course of doing the work of the decision paper ("means") and in the final alternatives, recommendations, and products ("ends.") This includes making very clear what is not in scope.

6. Objectives

How to Write the Objectives Section

The Objectives section describes the items that need to be attained, implemented, changed, or achieved. Decision papers are all about effecting positive change. The Objectives section is the key section that delineates that change; it ultimately defines success.

As with scope, objectives are defined for the analysis and general work in the course of developing the decision paper (means) *and* for the end products (ends). Just as with scope, the point here is that objectives have importance for the *means* and the *ends*. Remember, also, that the ends are ultimately achieved by the approval and actions to implement recommendations in the decision paper, after the decision paper is completed and approved.

Later, in the Alternatives and Recommendation section of your decision paper, you will propose solutions that meet the end-state objectives. In the final section, on Wrap-up, you will refer to the ends objectives and the means objectives and describe how they were met in the course of preparing and finalizing the decision paper (for the means objectives) and by implementing the recommendations (for the ends objectives). The connection (i.e., cross-reference) between the objectives and how they are satisfied in the Alternatives and Recommendation and Wrap-up sections needs to be clear and unambiguous. This is part of the *integrity* of the decision paper.

If the various constituencies, stakeholders, and rights holders cannot agree on objectives and/or you are having difficulty defining objectives, that is a strong sign that there is no point in developing the decision paper. Perhaps those commissioning a decision paper on a specific topic are pursuing a different agenda—anywhere from an innocent bias to a witch hunt, perhaps to make some organization, person, or team look bad. In any case, if you have difficulty defining objectives, then I advise consulting governance and considering whether to stop the decision paper development.

SMART Objectives

There is a school of thought that objectives need to be SMART, as in specific, measurable, achievable, relevant, and time-bound.[4] I would tend to agree, of course. It is always good to have such hard measures to let us know if our recommendations are successful. However, most of the time, objectives will need to include qualitative objectives, the success (or failure) of which is harder or impossible to measure. These qualitative objectives are often extremely important. For example, in the Strategies to Close the Lollipop Division decision paper, there could be an objective to "not alienate and in reality partner with and welcome more veteran employees who believe steadfastly that closing the lollipop product line is a mistake." This objective might be measured by the percentage of employees with a tenure of 10 years or greater who attend virtual town halls on the project. But this is more of an indicator than a hard measure. In any case, an objective that focuses on an area such as morale and spirit is important and should be included—even though it could be argued it is not SMART.

Objectives Hierarchy

I advise structuring objectives into a three-level hierarchy of Business, System, and Initiative. For decision papers that are developed to propose a project, the third level should be called "Project" instead of "Initiative." This structure operates as a hierarchy in that the business objectives have the highest priority, then system, and then initiative. Consider, for example, the objectives for the Rivertown Plant Explosion decision paper. A business objective to "improve the operational safety of our plants" would clearly be more important than an initiative objective to "complete final report in time for annual safety summit meeting."

In general, a higher-level objective can be achieved even if a lower-level objective is missed—but it does not make sense to do the opposite.

The wisdom of working to this hierarchy becomes clear when you imagine what it would be like to *not* follow the hierarchy. Imagine reporting

---

[4] Doran, G. T., *There's a S.M.A.R.T. Way to Write Management's Goals and Objectives.* (New York: Management Review, 1981). 70 (11): 35–36.

out at the Annual Safety Summit meeting that the decision paper was finalized and recommendations put forward, but they are incomplete—they were merely reported as complete because we needed to meet the deadline of having them ready by this meeting. Clearly an interim report should be made at the safety summit, with the actual work (to meet the business objective) continuing.

Working to this three-tier hierarchy also fits well with the distinction we are making between ends and means. Business and system objectives are ends objectives. They will be achieved by executing fully on the recommended option defined in the decision paper. Initiative Objectives can contain both ends and means objectives, but they have a primary focus on means.

Objectives Hierarchy

- <u>Business Objectives</u>. Describes the net effect of the end products but not the end products themselves. Achieving the business objectives is the definitive reason for taking on the decision paper process.

- <u>System Objectives</u>. Describes the physical, technical, or discrete characteristics of the end products. This includes changes in ongoing policy, organization, process, systems, equipment, or technology.

- <u>Initiative Objectives</u>. Describes characteristics of the initiative irrespective of what is being implemented. Typically, these are in the realm of working within a timeframe or with a limit on resources (budget, people, and material.) Initiative Objectives may describe the "ends" Initiative Objectives as well, typically on timeframes and resources.

There is a little trick to check that your objectives are complete and that they are correctly assigned to the right objective hierarchy. That is this:

- Going down the hierarchy, from Business to System to Initiative, answers the question "How?."

- Going up the hierarchy, from Initiative to System to Business, answers the question "Why?."

Let's try it: How will we improve the safe operation of our plants? Answer:

By making changes to policy, organization, process, systems, and technology. Why are we reporting our recommendations at the Annual Safety Summit? Answer: To improve the safe operation of our plants.

If there are holes in that logic, then you are likely missing objectives.

Accomplishing the business objectives is the ultimate goal. The challenge includes accomplishing the business objectives while also meeting the lower-priority system and Initiative Objectives. The Rivertown Plant Explosion decision paper may, for example, have a business objective of reducing the probability of future fatalities on the job to zero. And the Seattle Office Closing decision paper may have a business objective of retaining all Seattle office high-performing employees. The hows of these business objectives would be in the system and Initiative Objectives.

Goals vs. Objectives

This guide stays clear of (ignores, really) the distinction some make between goals and objectives. According to this school of thought, a goal is an outcome target that is broad and often long-term, while an objective is a specific and narrow target that, when combined with other objectives, results in achieving a goal or goals. I find this approach academically interesting but ultimately not useful in a practical setting. My overall guidance on this is to follow your organization's standard, if they call for a distinction between goals and objectives. But if such a standard is not imposed on you, ignore this structure and stick to the objectives three-level hierarchy defined in this guide. You will notice that the Business Objectives serve in a manner similar to what some might call goals. I say ignore this because I find no value-added "so what?" to this academic difference.

Political Misapplications

There is great risk when the development of Objectives is politicized, that is, when the process is subverted to serve less-than-pure motives and agendas. Misdirected objectives can throw the entire decision paper process off course, typically with very bad results. For example, consider the reasonable and forthright business objective, "Achieve a smooth, well-informed transition off of our lollipop product line for our major retail customers." What if political operators argued to add: ". . . acknowledging that we mishandled and mismanaged the product line." This may please those with motives to make people in the organization look like incompetents who "mismanaged" a key product line, but it has no place in the business objectives.

A way to manage this risk is for the decision paper leadership and DPAH to facilitate a rigorous process of objectives definition. Carefully review each draft objective to make sure it is free of bias and does not prejudge the findings and analysis yet to come. Objectives are forward-looking, not backward-blaming.

Summary

The Objectives section makes very clear what we plan to accomplish and according to what priority. Business and System objectives focus on the expected outcomes; initiative (also called project) objectives focus on the work that will be conducted to meet the business and system objectives. Objectives are followed on a strict hierarchy: business most important, then, in sequence, system and initiative.

7. Methodology

How to Write the Methodology Section

The Methodology section describes *how* the work required to execute the purpose of the decision paper will be conducted. Once again, we make the distinction between the methodology undertaken to develop the decision paper—the means—and the methodology proposed to act on the recommendations of the decision paper—the ends. They are two distinct things that must be explained separately within the Methodology section.

A task plan, with its inherent assignments, estimates, and critical paths, is one key component of the Methodology section, but it would be a serious mistake to view methodology as *only* the task plan. A task plan is generally good at identifying *what* needs to be done and *who* will be doing it, but it is lacking on *how* the work will be accomplished.

The Methodology section includes not just a task plan but also the approach, techniques, methods, instruments, and tools (automated or manual) that were used to develop the decision paper (means) and that will be used in the course of conducting the recommendations of the decision paper (ends).

An example of the means methodology for the Failed Financial Systems Project: The approach might include a structured questionnaire sent to all stakeholders and team members. The questionnaire would have multiple objectives, including gauging whether end users were sufficiently involved and sufficiently listened to, understanding anticipated benefits of the new system, understanding pain points of the existing system, and understanding whether the IT architecture team's role was well defined and executed to include necessary architecture features in the final system design.

The methodology, or how work will be done, is highly dependent on the subject area the decision paper is dealing with. For example, the Rivertown Plant Explosion decision paper may include, in its methodology, highly technical engineering design reviews, including metallurgical analysis. The Seattle Office Closing methodology would perhaps have financial and market analyses as part of its methodology.

Getting to *How*

For reasons that I have never been able to figure out, competent managers often find it very difficult to explain (either in writing or verbally) what methodology or approach they will take with their work. In my work as a CIO, for example, I would ask *how* the requirements for a new business system would be developed. The response I would often get was "We'll meet with the users." The fact of a meeting is a *what*; I was looking for a *how*. One plausible answer would be: "We will meet with the users and workshop through the key business processes, documenting them step by step and noting current areas of satisfaction and pain points." Yet another answer would be: "The Business Analysts will first develop logical data models and identify key process triggers, after which we will meet with the users to validate the data models and step through the processes [etc.]."

Table 3. Methodology Examples

Decision Paper	Methodology—Means	Methodology—Ends
Failed Financial Systems Project	• Structured questionnaire to all stakeholders and participants • Independent Architecture Review • Detailed Analysis of Bugs and Bug Fixes During Integration and User Testing • Review of key governance documentation, including Project Risk Assessment and Project Steering Committee Notes	• Changes to Project Policy • Changes to Project Quality Assurance Program • Changes to Major Projects Kickoff Process • Changes to roles and responsibilities for project governance • Updating Estimating Methodology and Calculations of Contingency for Schedule and Budget

Decision Paper	Methodology—Means	Methodology—Ends
	• Review of product selection process from requirements through to selection and contracting	• Changes to training and orientation for all IT project participants—including a dedicated core team and those outside the project but with project responsibilities.
Rivertown Plant Explosion	• Outside engineering lab review and stress testing of machinery metal casings	• Redevelopment of safety review practices for new plant machinery/ equipment • New employee equipment-specific certification requirements
Seattle Office Closing	• Financial analysis of Seattle office performance compared to home office locations for key financial metrics such as clients per professional	• New consolidated business case process for new business locations
Strategies to Close the Lollipop Division	• Structured interviews and Open Houses with the largest and most strategic existing customers to be affected by the product line termination	• New long-term strategic and financial plan requirements for all product lines, modeling viability for the long term

Political Misapplications

You will find in less mature or less healthy organizational cultures that there will be attempts to add and/or remove items from the Methodology section with the aim of skewing the findings or obscuring some details. For example, a person who knows that, despite being identified as a "key user" of the new system, they themselves did hardly any work on the Failed Financial Systems may want to exclude the "key user time on project" analysis from the methodology.

While the phrase *sacred cow* is a bit trite, it is very useful in identifying another political misapplication: attempts to exclude or insulate long-standing policies or practices from any changes. To avoid this pitfall, state early in the launch of the decision paper initiative that all options are on the table; there will be no sacred cows when it comes to the findings and recommendations of the decision paper.

Summary

The Methodology section makes very clear *how* we prepare the decision paper (means) and *how* we plan to accomplish the recommendations put forward in the decision paper (ends). Methodology gets into the techniques, practices, and tools (manual and automated) that will be employed.

8. Constraints, Assumptions and Dependencies

How to Write the Constraints, Assumptions and Dependencies Section

The Constraints, Assumptions and Dependencies (CAD) section shapes and, in some ways, limits the work you can do and the recommendations you can make.

- Constraints. These are items that limit the possible work, findings, analyses, and recommendations. Constraints have the characteristic of being insurmountable. For example, the time zone difference between the UK firm that produced some of the key assemblies used in the equipment at the Rivertown Plant and the Western Canadian offices impeded the ability for the teams to collaborate, as they only shared working hours for one hour a day. Another example: "The governmental work safety authority requires an analysis of the root causes within 90 days of safety events with the characteristics of the Rivertown Plant incident." Both of these are constraints. They cannot be managed away; they cannot be worked around; they cannot be ignored.

  If you think something may be a constraint, but it can be achieved (perhaps with great effort or the expenditure of much political capital), then it is not truly a constraint. For example, "The Northwest Regional VP, as the Project Sponsor, did not want to ask the board for more time to bring the Seattle office to profitability" is not a constraint. The Project Sponsor could have asked the board for more time but just decided not to.

  Constraints are typically from outside governance entities or are a characteristic of nature. Decision papers often document very few constraints and sometimes no constraints at all.

  It is useful to document constraints in a table that shows the constraints in column A, the effect on the decision paper preparation (means) in column B, and the effect on the recommendations in column C.

- <u>Assumptions</u>. Assumptions are considered true for planning purposes and are clearly documented. These may be better phrased as "working assumptions" in that the work to prepare the decision paper and/or execute the recommendations of the decision paper will proceed (without hesitation) as if the assumptions were true. But we will go with "assumptions" in this guide.

  Assumptions are things that affect (impede or facilitate) your work and that are reasonable to take as true and/or given. There is an inherent expectation that assumptions will not meaningfully change. Assumptions can be reasonably thought to exist even though it is possible they will be removed or altered. For example, for Strategies to Close the Lollipop Division, there is an assumption that the cost of product ingredients, particularly cane sugar, will continue along its general 20-year trend. This is a working assumption that may be proven false if, for example, prices rise or drop dramatically shortly after the decision paper analysis. Regardless, this is a reasonable assumption, sufficiently documented, that allows the work to proceed.

  Assumptions, well documented, are a good way to avoid analysis paralysis.

  As with constraints, it is useful to document assumptions in a table that shows the assumptions in column A, the effect on the decision paper preparation (means) in column B, and the effect on the recommendations in column C.

- <u>Dependencies</u>. Dependencies are tasks, actions, and decisions required to be made *before* the finalization of the decision paper (means) or before the execution of recommendations (ends). Just as with Constraints, Dependencies have the characteristic of being insurmountable. There is no such thing as a "nice to have" Dependency. For example, the Failed Financial Systems Project decision paper may have several dependencies: Full access to project documentation library, full access to meet with key project personnel, and full access to exit interviews for key team leaders who quit during the course of the project would all be valid dependencies.

Dependencies must truly adhere to the notion that they are required in order to prepare the decision paper and/or to execute the recommendations. If there are reasonable workarounds, then these are not dependencies. They are part of the methodology or approach. An easy test to determine if you are dealing with an actual dependency is to ask yourself, "Can I reasonably proceed without this documentation, task, action, or decision?" If the answer is no, then you have a dependency.

It then goes without saying that if dependencies are not provided, the work of the decision paper preparation and/or recommendation implementation cannot proceed.

It is useful to document dependencies in a table that shows the dependencies in column A, the effect on the decision paper preparation (means) in column B, and the effect on the recommendation in column C.

Political Misapplications

As the author of the decision paper, one of your jobs is to make sure the Constraints, Assumptions and Dependencies are put forward and documented completely, without unnecessary embellishment, and without hidden agendas. However, you will find in less mature or less healthy organizational cultures that Constraints, Assumptions, and Dependencies get used as weapons to drive an agenda or to kill off the entire initiative. There is not much advice I can provide in these situations except to argue on the side of facts, evidence, and logic. For example, one with impure motives may argue that the dependency "access to interview project audit personnel" be removed from the Failed Financial Systems Project decision paper since they know the project audit function missed key signs of the project being in trouble. Use the governance structure to *fight these battles* against those attempting to subvert a forthright documentation of Constraints, Assumptions and Dependencies.

Summary

The Constraints, Assumptions, and Dependencies sections document relevant and important information about the environment in which the decision paper is being developed and the environment in which the decision paper's recommendations will be executed. Sponsors, stakeholders and rights holders are well served when they understand the hard limitations (constraints), reasonable givens (assumptions), and necessary prerequisites (dependencies) of the decision paper initiative. Courage and forthrightness are needed to ensure the relevant and important constraints, assumptions and dependencies are documented, and not suppressed or distorted for political or selfish reasons.

9. Issues

How to Write the Issues Section

Issue identification must be well controlled, or the list of issues will be voluminous and pointless to try to manage. To help in the productive identification of a tightly defined list of issues, I offer this definition of what an issue is and what it is not.

An issue is one of two things:

- A problem that must be solved for which there is not yet a feasible solution; or

- A decision that must be made about which the relevant decision makers are not in agreement.

An issue is *not*:

- A very complex, difficult, or important thing that must be done. Such things are actions or task plan actions, and they are addressed in the decision paper sections on Methodology and Risks.

- The correct way to document and recognize a Risk that has manifested. (See Risk section discussion.) Risks that manifest *do* need to be dealt with, but they are not Issues.

- A way to make a political statement about an aspect of the project someone disagrees with.

- A way to re-open closed decisions and/or keep accepted risks up for eternal debate.

- A way to get "asks" into the project that had heretofore not been in scope.

Issues may pertain to the development of the decision paper (means) or the recommendations (ends.)

Consider an Issue example: The decision paper on Strategies to Close the Lollipop Division may have an issue as to whether to pursue selling the business to their major competitors. It may be that the executive team is evenly split on this consideration and the CEO is unsure. Yet, for the work to proceed, it is necessary to know whether such a strategy is part of the plan.

For another example, consider the issue in the Failed Financial Systems Project as to whether the review scope includes the company's Cloud Migration Strategy. Again, key decision makers, stakeholders and rights holders may be evenly split on this. Yet, for the work to proceed, a fundamental question of scope such as this must be decided.

It is useful to document issues in a table (called an Issue Log) that shows the issues in column A, their effects on the decision paper preparation (means) in column B, and their effects on the recommendations in column C. Issues should be sequentially and uniquely numbered. It may be useful to add a column D for "potential resolutions" as a way to document the decisions that might be made that will lead to closing the issue.

Political Misapplications

You will find in less mature or less healthy organizational cultures that Issues are mismanaged and/or misused.

- Not an Issue, But Important. An atmosphere may develop in which if something is not tracked as an Issue, then some key people question whether it is getting sufficient attention. For example, the Failed Financial Systems Project paper may have decided that User and Performance Test standards and tool sets are in scope. But some who want to make a great show of this may ask for an issue that states, "User and performance test standards may have been inadequate for a project of this size, complexity and strategic operational importance." There is likely some truth to this statement. However, nothing is *at issue;* it does not belong on the issue log.

- Issues Lead to Issue Tracking. That having issues then leads to issue tracking makes sense. Be aware that, once identified, Issues take on a life (cycle) of their own. It is very likely, for example, that regular status meetings on the subject of the decision paper will include a standard topic called "Issue Status" or "Issue Tracking." That is good as long as it does not become a substitute for overall status and progress reporting. Reporting on the status of issues is no substitute for a holistic review of progress. It would be an anecdotal way of reporting rather than a systemic, holistic way of reporting. Spending disproportionate amount of time on Issue Tracking over status monitoring can also create the impression that everything is problematic (i.e., "at issue") since issues are the dominant subject under discussion.

- <u>Adding Non-Issues</u>. Be careful that Issue logs do not become a way for some constituents to drop in ad-hoc asks that have no place in the Issue list and may have no place in the decision paper analysis at all. This is a way people try to use Issue management to commandeer the subject of the decision paper and to send it off in directions that may not be helpful. For example, some may be unhappy with the exempt (i.e., non-union) employee overtime policy at the Rivertown Plant and want that tracked as an issue; even though it was well established that it is not relevant to the plant explosion analysis and is therefore not part of the scope of the analysis.

- <u>Issues as Signs of Failure</u>. Some may view the existence of issues as evidence of the failure of management. In this scenario, some may argue that there should be no issues, now or perhaps ever. "We are all working on this together, right? There are no issues." This approach should be dismissed, and the two-level definition of Issue (described earlier) should be followed. To build a healthy culture, be careful not to demonize the existence of issues. Whether there are many or few issues says nothing good or bad about the subject of the decision paper or the decision paper development itself.

One way to ensure issues do not proliferate to include many non-issues is to have a rule that issues may only be added to the issue log on the approval of the DPAH leadership.

Summary

The Issues section documents resolvable items that are *at issue* in that they must be resolved in order to achieve the goals of the decision paper, but they are as yet still open. Beware and guard against the misuse of Issues for self-serving or political ends.

10. Risks

How to Write the Risks Section

It is not possible to eliminate risk; risks must be identified, assessed, and managed. You need to *identify* and *assess* risks in a way that is systematic and provides some assurance of completeness. This risk *identification* and *assessment* is included in this decision paper section on Risks. That is followed by developing approaches for preventing the risks from manifesting, mitigating the damage should the risks manifest, and recovering from the harm after the source of the risk is either accepted or mitigated. The approaches to prevent, mitigate, and recover are listed at a high level in the decision paper section on Risks. But the work to follow through, to manage risks, is largely in the Methodology section. Risk management approaches and steps are integrated into the Methodology section along with other work to get the goals of the decision paper scope completed.

Defining Risks

A massive trove of material exists on risks and risk management. ISO 31000 defines risk as "the effect of uncertainty on objectives."[5] Risk expert, H. Felix Kloman, defines risk as "a measure of the probable likelihood, consequences, and timing of a future event."[6] Another expert, Ortwin Renn, makes note of risk being "the possibility that an undesirable state of reality (adverse effects) may occur."[7] Norman Marks, in his excellent book *World-Class Risk Management*, says, "Uncertainty lies between where we are and where we want to go."[8] Overall, Marks considers the management of risk to be about understanding and dealing

---

[5] International Organization for Standardization, *Risk Management—Guidelines*, 2nd ed., ISO 31000:2018(en) (Paris: ISO, 2018), 3.1.

[6] H. Felix Kloman, *The Fantods of Risk: Essays on Risk Management* (Lyme, Connecticut: Seawrack Press, 2008), 12.

[7] Ortwin Renn, *Risk Governance: Coping with Uncertainty in a Complex World* (London: Earthscan, 2008), 1.

[8] Norman Marks, *World-Class Risk Management* (self-pub., CreateSpace, 2015), 17.

with uncertainty—dealing with the possibility that events may manifest as obstacles to achieving stated objectives and, therefore, goals.

Many of these sources on risk and risk management include in their definition of risk the consideration that risks encompass both the uncertainty of positive/good outcomes as well as uncertainty of negative/bad outcomes. I disagree and advise that risks be identified only when there is a possibility of a negative or bad outcome. While there is some intellectual completeness to considering both positive and negative risks, there is very little benefit from time spent considering events or decisions that may positively influence the subject of the decision paper analysis.

Borrowing from Renn, the definition of risk I use in this guide is "the assessment and analysis of future possible undesirable states of reality occurring that impede or prevent the attainment of stated objectives." Note that the likelihood that the risk will manifest is not relevant to this definition of risk, or to your process of risk identification.

Risk of Ends, Not Means

Because risks, by definition, refer to *future* events that may present obstacles in achieving objectives, the Risks section of the decision paper relates to the ends only, not the means. Your Risks section is therefore looking at the effect of uncertainty on the successful execution of the *outcome* recommendations. This means we are taking as given (in our language, we have an *assumption*) that whatever risks were present in the decision paper preparation process that affected achieving a thorough and high-quality paper have been dealt with.

What then, you may wonder, is to be done with uncertainties encountered during the preparation of the decision paper? In most situations, such uncertainties are documented in the Constraints section. For example, the Rivertown Plant Explosion decision paper may raise a question as to whether the video recorders for some of the CCTV cameras malfunctioned, as Plant Operations reported, or were secretly and deliberately disabled by Operations or Safety personnel. This may never be known. The decision paper may include this uncertainty as a constraint to acknowledge and record that this item will never be fully resolved, but the paper moves on with its analysis and recommendations notwithstanding.

A simple rule for decision papers: Uncertainty about the past is a Constraint or Assumption; uncertainty about the future is a Risk.

Completeness

The greatest challenge for those writing the Risks section of decision papers and endeavoring to have an appropriately useful delineation of risks is the question of completeness. It is relatively easy to identify a list of risks while brainstorming or ideating in another ad-hoc manner. It is another matter to have confidence that the risks you have identified represent the entire important set of what-ifs that need to be considered and managed. Please do not misunderstand me, it *is* useful to gather relevant constituents, stakeholders, and rights holders and brainstorm the topic of risks. However, that is not a substitute for a process that will ensure completeness. Depending on the subject area of your decision paper, there are two approaches to completeness that I would recommend. Both require workshops with key individuals involved.

- Risk Completeness Model 1: Follow the Life Cycle. This approach involves facilitated workshops with all relevant constituents. Step through the execution of the recommendations, and determine what uncertainties (i.e., risks) threaten its successful execution. If it's useful, as you step through the recommendations, prompt for risks by functional area: Finance, IT, Operations, Safety, Audit, Facilities, etc.

- Risk Completeness Model 2: Risk Objects. The central concept behind the Risk Objects approach is that risks are present where objects (i.e., nouns, things) are present. You can list the major categories of Risk Objects relevant to the scope of your decision paper, then workshop through what the risks are. For example, the Failed Financial Systems Project would have risk objects of server technology, software, software customizations, databases, servers, information security architecture, users, vendors, training materials, project team members, etc. Sometimes it is easier to identify risks when you start with an exhaustive (but high-level) list of the risk objects than it would be to identify all the risks ad hoc.

Risks Section

The risks should be stated in full sentences to clearly explain what is "at risk." The wording should clearly explain the cause and effect of the risk manifesting. For example, it would be better to word a risk as "There is a risk that, despite all feasible improvements in plant safety, company insurers will not underwrite a policy, effectively shutting down operations at Rivertown Plant" than to say "Insurance underwriting risk." The latter just leaves too much up to the reader to figure out. If most of the risk descriptions are long as a result of making them full sentences, it's okay to provide a caption. In our example, the caption could be "Insurance Underwriting:" and then the complete sentence.

It is useful to document Risks in a table that shows the risk statements in column A. Risks should be sequentially and uniquely numbered to make referencing back to them easier. Columns B, C and D would contain risk management approaches to B) Prevent, C) Detect, and D) Remedy the risk. The Prevent column may be called "Prevent/Avoid"; the Remedy column may be called "Remedy and Recover." Note the mini lifecycle that emerges as columns B, C, and D step through time: first, try to prevent the risk from manifesting; failing that, find a way to detect the manifestation of the risk; and failing that, find a way to remedy and recover the outcomes of the risk manifesting. As with the risk statements, Prevent, Detect, and Remedy are best explained using complete sentences.

A reasonable approach to managing some risks is to look to share the risk, as with the engagement of insurers, or to understand and accept the risk. Either way, it's possible that not much will be done to reduce the likelihood of the risk manifesting. With that in mind, optionally, columns E and F could be added to the Risk table to note E) Risk Sharing and F) Risk Acceptance. This will depend on the nature of the decision paper's scope and analysis. Risk Sharing could also be called" Risk Sharing / Risk Transfer."

Risks Defined; Now What?

Once you have completed the Risk section and table of the decision paper, you are not done with risks in the decision paper. The process of identifying and articulating risks for the decision paper preparation includes adding detail to other sections of the decision paper to manage the risks so identified. The heavy work is done in the Methodology section, where work, controls, and approaches are defined that will help prevent, detect, and remedy risks. You may also find yourself updating Constraints and Assumptions to facilitate managing risks. Overall, you are circling back to these earlier sections as invariably the process and results of identifying risks alter the work to be done and the constraints to be identified.

Presuming that your recommendation is supported and the work (after the approval of the decision paper) proceeds, more detailed risk management is practiced. We do not delve into that post-decision-paper state, but consider that risk management during execution will include further risk evaluation, and an assessment of risk appetite and risk tolerance. Per the Committee of Sponsoring Organizations of the Treadway Commission (COSO), risk appetite is the amount of risk an organization is willing to accept. Risk tolerance represents the application of risk appetite to specific objectives. And during the execution of the approved recommendation, the owners of each risk will be clearly communicated.

Political Misapplications

You will find in less mature or less healthy organizational cultures that there will be attempts to undermine the risk identification and risk management process. In my experience, most of these efforts will be based on the mistaken and unhealthy view that the mere statement of a risk is an accusation that must be thwarted or repressed. A way to manage this is to include a summary of the rationale for the risk analysis—emphasizing that this is a normal part of all decision paper analyses—at the start of the risk workshops.

Summary

The Risks section documents potential events that may impede or prevent the attainment of the decision paper's stated objectives. The emphasis is on risk identification. Risk management is largely handled in the Methodology section and in the execution of the recommendations.

11. Findings

Logic Trail: Findings to Recommendation

Beginning with Findings, the next four sections have a tight logical relationship which you as the author of the decision paper must keep top of mind so that the paper will have logical integrity and therefore credibility. Your Findings lead to your Analysis, which in turn leads to your Conclusions, which in turn lead to a set of Alternatives. The final step is the Recommendation, which is a specific recommendation to implement one or more of the Alternatives. Each of these sections has its logical foundations set in the preceding sections. I will explain each individually, beginning with Findings.

How to Write the Findings Section

Findings are the delineation of the facts and evidence discovered and presented for consideration. Findings are raw data, presented without conclusion, without analysis, without interpretation, without editorializations. You will see that you use very few adjectives and adverbs in the Findings section, as Findings are simply nouns. As David Byrne sings, "Facts are simple and facts are straight."[9]

Be mindful that the findings must be relevant to the scope of the decision paper analysis. There is no point in discussing the climate differences between Seattle, Toronto, and San Francisco if that bears no relevance at all to the Seattle Office Closing analysis. But it is okay to present findings that later are determined to be irrelevant. That is in itself interesting and can be noted in the Conclusions section.

You will *find* that some of the work being reviewed within the scope of the decision paper went well and some of it did not. Sometimes the intent, planning, and preparations were on target, but the execution fails. In other words: Any good idea can be poorly implemented. In preparing the Findings section, you will need to show very clearly what went well and what did not. Even if what you are analyzing is a failure

---

[9] Talking Heads, "Crosseyed and Painless," vinyl recording, *Remain in Light* (Sire, 1980).

(examples: the Rivertown and Financial Systems decision papers), you will still find some correct plans and actions. They should be "found" along with the mistakes and missteps.

Sensitivity

People are delicate, political beings. Often when someone is presented with a fact (i.e., a finding) that may be interpreted as making them look incompetent, unreasonable, or ignorant, they will react emotionally rather than intellectually. That is our nature. Given that, we must write decision papers that contain some sensitivity to these emotions. One way to handle this is to avoid any direct statement or even an implication of intent. Realize that you cannot possibly understand motive, you can only understand action, inaction, result, and repercussion. In other words, stick to the findings and do not interpret when completing the Findings section. This approach is more sensitive to people's feelings.

Organizing Findings

Findings are organized by logical topical areas. The Findings section often includes quantifiable data in tables. If the tables of data go on for pages, they are often included as appendices, but they are always referenced from the Findings section. Consider possible Findings for our sample decision papers in Table 4:

Table 4. Findings Examples

Decision Paper	Findings
Failed Financial Systems Project	• Tables of bugs identified and listed by testing phase, noting average time to remediate • Table of team members showing home organization, duration on project, and project phases they worked on

Decision Paper	Findings

	• Summary of interview notes on:
	  ○ What went well
	  ○ What did not go well
	  ○ Recommendations for improvement
	• Results of dry-run conversions, including G/L balancing
	• Summary of Internal Audit review findings and management actions prior to go-live

Rivertown Plant Explosion	• Review of site reports from Safety Officer • Review of inspection reports logged up to a year prior to the incident • Summary of notes from interviews with all managers and workers on site on the day of the event, including those survivors who were injured • Review of post-event report conducted by OEM that was the source of the equipment that malfunctioned, causing the incident
Seattle Office Closing	• Review of office performance reporting, including new and lost clients, financial performance, sales targets vs. actual, etc. • Review of absenteeism and sick time taken in the Seattle office in comparison to the other US and Canadian offices • Summary of interview notes for cross-selection of management and other employees assigned to the Seattle office
Strategies to Close the Lollipop Division	• Review of product performance reports company-wide, comparing the Lollipop Division to other product lines in key measures such as cost of goods sold, margin, profit/loss, product recalls, etc.

Decision Paper	Findings
	• Summary of customer survey gauging reactions to the potential closure of the lollipop product line

Qualitative Findings

Some findings are impossible to turn into numerical data. To the extent that they are relevant, they still must be included and described in the Findings. In these cases of qualitative findings, just describe them as neutrally as possible. For example, for the Failed Financial Systems Project decision paper, you may find that the HR department noted an increase in IT employees looking for alternative employment outside the company. But this would be related as an anecdote, as there is no data on employees who look externally but do not actually resign. The finding you document with this example is that the HR department has stated they observed an increase in IT employees looking for alternative employment.

Findings of Experts

Often some of the findings come from experts who have been asked to look into the situation and have documented their *findings*. You would formally obtain the expert findings, cite them, note the source, and take no view either way as to whether there is agreement or not with the findings. Consider for example if the Board of Directors hired an outside law firm to see if laws governing factory safety were violated at the Rivertown Plant. This is indeed relevant to the decision paper; the conclusions of this report should be included in the Findings section. Just be sure to attribute the findings to the law firm—by name—and take no position yourself. In this example, the citation may be: "Big Deal Lawyer Firm's report stated that their view was that no local or federal safety laws were violated." You can then note where to find the report.

Political Misapplications

You will find in less mature or less healthy organizational cultures that some people will argue with Findings. They may accuse the preparers of the decision paper of a "set-up" if they see findings that appear to clearly point to logical conclusions that put them in a bad light. A politically expedient approach for such individuals is to discredit the underlying data. There is only one approach I have found to be effective in dealing with such individuals, and that is to keep the Findings impeccably pure. They should contain only data and information that are plainly stated, supported by hard evidence, and impossible to argue with. This is important in any case because the Findings are the groundwork upon which the Analysis, Conclusions and Recommendation sections are built. This is another reason I do not advocate combining the Findings section with another section, producing a dual-purpose section such as "Findings and Analysis" or "Findings and Recommendation." As the authors walk through the decision paper with such detractors and politically motivated individuals, you can pause at the end of Findings to ensure everyone is on board with these basic statements of fact.

Summary

The Findings section delineates the relevant facts and evidence discovered and presented for consideration. The data and information presented are not analyzed in any way in the Findings section; they are stated blandly in order to provide the foundation for a logical progression to analysis, conclusions, alternatives and recommendations. Use appendices to include voluminous findings, but summarize them in the Findings section.

12. Analysis

How to Write the Analysis Section

With Findings established as the foundation, Analysis is where you think through and articulate what the findings mean. Analysis is subjective and conjectural, the result of deductive reasoning; findings are not. Here is where you as the writer of the decision paper (and whatever team you are working with) add great value. Analysis draws on the skills of analytical thinking and synthesizing data to learn what it all means. Analysis does not include drawing conclusions or proposing alternatives. The Analysis section presents what is interesting and enlightening and stops there.

With the example of the Failed Financial Systems Project, the Analysis may note the findings that User Testing identified a smaller number of software defects than normal for such a project during a time frame when expert users were participating inconsistently because several were pulled on and then off a few times in order to handle normal (non-project) Finance workloads. One analysis of these findings would be that User Testing, while recognized as critical to the success of the project, was understaffed, improperly staffed, and not given the focus and attention necessary for such a project. This analysis has many implications, just one of which is that it makes it easier to understand another finding: the finding that the User Test standards, methods, and practices likely were sufficiently robust and detailed for a project this size and that the key problem was flawed execution.

Some techniques you can use in developing the Analysis:

- Look for anomalies in the Findings. This is data out of normal ranges and/or data indicating unusual activities or events. But be careful: often you have to look beyond the cursory analysis to more intricate and subtle explanations for the anomalies.

- Look for times the data shows something was not done that should have been. Besides looking at the effect this had on the initiative, ask why such a thing could have been missed.

- Look for areas where lower-level objectives were given primacy over higher-level (i.e., more important) objectives. Was equipment rushed into service at Rivertown without adequate safety review to meet raised production targets? In this example, meeting production targets, an initiative objective, was given primacy over safety, a business objective.

- For problem-oriented decision papers, do a walk-back analysis, in which you look at the *bad* outcomes and ask "why did that happen?"

In each of these techniques the data is *speaking* to you. Listen to it; listen to the findings and data without being distracted by politics, and you will have a high-quality Analysis section.

Political Misapplications

There are a few pitfalls to avoid when politics meets a decision paper Analysis section.

Some authors replace the thoughtful analysis needed with a tour of relevant executives and the transcription of what each executive thinks the analysis is. Such decision paper authors can misunderstand and/or undermine what they are really doing with the preparation of the decision paper, especially in the Analysis section. This is highly dangerous in that it undermines the entire logical structured decision paper process. If decisions were just going to be made by management fiat, the entire decision paper process could have just been skipped. That would not be a great result, but it would be better and more honest than pretending to follow a rigorous process.

As you recall from our discussion of the Need section, aside from those decision papers required by mandate or for continuous improvement, decision papers are often either problem-focused, such as with our examples of the Financial Systems Project and Rivertown Plant papers, or opportunity-focused, such as with the Strategies to Close the Lollipop Division paper. Some can be both. Either way, the Analysis section is likely to find some organizational entities either did not do their job or did not do their job well. Consider how perceptions will change regarding someone who wrote a glowing, optimistic 5-year plan for the Lollipop Division just two years ago when there is a paper all about shutting down that business line. The decision paper Analysis section will likely analyze why growth and/or profit targets were not achieved. I don't like looking at it this way, but decision papers identify winners and losers. They don't do this on purpose, but they do it in the course of thoroughly laying out the work of a decision paper. Given that, there is often political pressure to not make anyone look bad. From a human standpoint, this is understandable. However, my advice is to resist this pressure. The story needs to be laid out logically, irrespective of whether some constituencies will look bad.

Summary

The Analysis section takes the findings as input and then, with the Objectives in mind, presents an analysis of what the findings mean. This is a value-added step by the team preparing the decision paper. It requires thoughtfulness, creativity, and courage.

13. Conclusions

How to Write the Conclusions Section

With Findings established as the foundation and Analysis saying what the Findings mean, the Conclusions section takes the leap to synthesize the analysis work holistically and draw a prioritized set of conclusions. For problem-oriented decision papers, these conclusions solve root causes in all their richness, multidimensionality, and complexity. For opportunity-oriented and continuous improvement decision papers, conclusions draw clear paths to success in the form of prioritized next steps to best achieve the benefits of the opportunity.

A hallmark of a good Conclusions section is that it makes judgments and goes out on a limb to state logical conclusions given all the data (i.e., findings) and analysis to-date. Not all of the judgments made will have the force and logic of a mathematical proof. Most Conclusions sections take a line of thought (i.e., inductive reasoning) that could reasonably be challenged. For example, a Rivertown Plant Explosion decision paper that concludes closing the plant would have almost no benefits and is not an option to be recommended could reasonably be argued with. In any case, this example would indicate the decision paper authors weighed, evaluated and thought through all the findings, and analyses and reached reasonable conclusions.

A good Conclusions section is the antidote to "analysis paralysis." The paper presents a reasoned and responsible synthesis of all information gathered to-date and makes concrete recommendations—recommendations that can be acted on.

Those who are overly shy or timid should frankly not be authors of Conclusions sections. There is no point in presenting interesting, bold, and potentially controversial conclusions if the authors are going to back away from them when challenged. One way I recommend dealing with a cultural environment that makes bold conclusions uncredible when coming from any source other than the CEO's office is to handle this directly when previewing the decision paper at the highest levels, before it is finalized. See the discussion of Iterations and Review in this guide.

Political Misapplications

As I have said, there will be winners and losers after a decision paper is presented, even when that is not the goal of the paper. Any document that recommends change will be in that arena. Many cultures give unofficial permission to organizational groups and/or individuals to reject conclusions that put them in a bad light. The only way to deal with this is to not deal with it. Put your conclusions out there and deal with the political pressure when it happens. Perhaps discuss this aspect deliberately with the approval/governance entities during the draft iterations and finalization stages.

Summary

The Conclusions section takes the bold and creative step of drawing conclusions directly relevant to the scope and objectives of the decision paper. Conclusions are invariably subjective; it is possible that another team looking at the same findings and analyses would have drawn different conclusions.

14. Alternatives and Recommendation

How to Write the Alternatives and Recommendation Section

The decision paper exists to propose action—action that stands the integrity test in that it leads logically from all the prior sections of the decision paper. There is almost always a range of ways to proceed. This section of a decision paper presents a range of alternatives, then recommends just one.

Make your Alternatives and Recommendation section practical and actionable. Wish-list items have no place in this section. Do not include any alternative that is not achievable. This may seem so obvious that you may wonder why I am stating it. I say it because I have seen decision paper authors pressured into including alternatives that are not doable. Don't ever agree to run the 2-minute mile; it cannot be done.

Be very clear on rough estimates of costs (both one-time and ongoing), the actors and others in responsible roles, the timetables, and, most important, the expected outcomes.

The range of alternatives presented in this section of a decision paper typically includes some or substantially all of the following:

- Do Nothing. This is more aptly described as "continue business as usual." Accept whatever risk the problem presents or forego any action to seize a new opportunity.

- Do The Minimum. For situations where action is necessary, this alternative answers the question "What is the minimum we need to do?" Some stated objectives will not be achieved.

- Do What Has Been Proven. This alternative is restricted to approaches and methods that have been tried before and were successful. A low-risk option. Also, low innovation.

- Do Something Unproven. New approaches will be pioneered. Often this is the creative or inventive option. Higher risk than the Proven option.

- Implement A Full Solution. This is an ambitious and complete plan to address all areas of scope. All stated objectives will be achieved.

- <u>Outsource</u>. Includes moving some services or operations to an external partner.

- <u>Insource</u>. Some or all of the solutions will be done with internal resources, in facilities controlled by the organization.

- <u>Service Or Product Termination / Sunset</u>. This is the shutdown option. Close the service or business line. This alternative outlines how that will be done. Often, few of the objectives will be achieved.

I strongly recommend that a decision paper put just one alternative forward as the recommendation. Many writers, especially ones who are afraid to make a bold recommendation, conclude their decision papers with the statement that several alternatives are feasible and it is now up to senior decision makers to select one. Making a recommendation is a key step in the decision paper development process. If you dodge this duty, you are simply abdicating it to people who are less involved in the details than are the members of the Decision Paper Ad Hoc team.

When presenting Alternatives, include subsections for each alternative:

- Objectives Matrix
  - Business objectives
  - System objectives
  - Initiative or project objectives
- Issues resolution
- Work approach
- High level plan / schedule
- Benefits, both quantitative and qualitative
- Outcomes: policy, technology, process, organization
- Responsibility assignment matrix (RACI)
- Objectives matrix
- Costs, both one-time and ongoing

The Alternatives and Recommendation section is future-focused. Only refer to the past when it is helpful to fully understand the alternatives.

Note that the Objectives Matrix part of each Alternative should cross-reference the decision paper's *ends* objectives to the alternative. This is the ultimate scorecard for the effectiveness of an alternative: how well it can satisfy the stated objectives. The Issues Resolution table closes the issues identified earlier in the Issues section. Closure is either by definitive decision or resolution, or, for issues that remain unresolved, with a working assumption to be carried into the follow-on work of executing the recommended alternative.

Develop cost estimates for each alternative, including, of course, the recommended alternative. The precision and detail required for these cost estimates will depend on the need addressed by your decision paper. I advise keeping the cost estimates in the decision paper as high level as possible. Leave the detailed estimating to the team that will execute on the recommended alternative.

The recommendation being made in the decision paper is a beginning. It should be articulated to the level that you convey all key aspects of the recommendation, but it is not a complete plan. Avoid the temptation to create a full plan in the decision paper Recommendation section. That work is for another time, after the recommendation is approved (presumably).

Political Misapplications

Those with less than pure intentions have had many opportunities to undermine and disrupt the decision paper process during the preparations of the prior sections of the paper. If they have not succeeded by the time alternatives and recommendations are put forward, there are still a few tactics they can employy:

- <u>Lying In Agreement</u>. One tactic that is surprisingly effective is to verbalize or otherwise go on record as supporting the recommended alternative but then do nothing, or, worse, create obstacles to the success of following through on the recommendation. To deal with this tactic, it is often useful to continue to have strategic meetings with important senior sponsors so that anyone that is obstructing can be revealed. Or perhaps even better, those with such motives may abandon lying in agreement when it becomes clear they will be at open forums where their actions (or inactions) will be apparent to all involved.

- Bureaucratic Delays. This tactic involves using one's influence to procedurally delay the recommendation's next steps. For example, to implement the recommendations for the Failed Financial Systems Project decision paper, the changes to user assignment for testing will require updates to the project policy. Someone might argue that they are fully supportive of such changes, just so everyone knows that the project policy is updated every other year.

- Pretending No Closure. I marvel that this tactic exists. If I had not seen it with my own eyes many times, I would wonder how it could ever be effective. But it exists; I have seen it employed successfully. This tactic involves going to subsequent meetings and forums and stating that the recommendations cannot be acted on because of some obscure objection or contrived prerequisite. For example, someone may hold up the recommended actions to close the Lollipop Division by stating that clearly it would first need to be discussed at the annual shareholders' meeting, which is not for another nine months. Often this delay is accompanied by parallel steps to undo the approval of the recommendation.

With these last-ditch efforts to undermine the decision paper, forewarned is forearmed. As well, make sure the recommended alternative is supported by the organization's decision makers and that their support gets communicated widely and officially.

Summary

In the Alternatives and Recommendation section, the decision paper authors propose reasonable and actionable alternative ways forward, with cross-references back to the objectives. Then one of the alternatives is offered as a recommendation. Be careful not to develop a complete executable plan for the alternatives; that is more efficiently and effectively done after the recommended alternative is approved.

15. Wrap-up

How to Write the Wrap-up Section

The Wrap-up section's primary purpose is to present (usually with tables) an analysis of how well and how completely this decision paper addressed the stated areas of Scope, Objectives, and Issues. This is a simple but powerful section. It is part of the wisdom of telling your readers what you are going to do, doing it, and validating that it was done.

I advise making this section as boring as possible. It is not a recap; it is not a summary. No new ideas or data will be introduced. It is not there to re-sell the other sections of the decision paper. It is an accounting of completeness to wrap up the paper. With this section, your decision paper ends with a closed-loop integrity check that you did what you set out to do.

For Scope means and Objectives means, the table will list those items provided earlier with a checklist and minor commentary on how each was met in the course of producing the decision paper. For Scope ends and Objectives ends, the tables list each recommendation (including the one that is preferred) from the Alternatives and Recommendation section, and a checklist on whether and how each one addresses the stated objectives. It is common for some bare-bones recommendations to not meet all or many of the stated scope and objectives.

Column A of the table should be the scope and objectives items reproduced verbatim. Column B can be Full / Partial / Not Addressed to indicate whether the work was done. Column C can be a brief text commentary. "Not Addressed" is there for those cases where the scope and objectives items were not addressed. The Wrap-up table should briefly explain that and explain why it is not material to the work (means) and the ultimate recommendation (ends).

For Issues, the table can be a simple list of the issues provided earlier, with their disposition in text. The text commentary will likely include some discussion as to how the various alternatives address the previously open issues.

Political Misapplications

You will find in less mature or less healthy organizational cultures that some will argue with the details in the Wrap-up section. The best approach in that case is to be squeaky clean with the analysis. Do not overstate or exaggerate to say scope and/or objective items were met when arguably they have not been met. Do not say issues are resolved when they are still open. I also advise not really engaging with this game. If you keep the Wrap-up section tightly grounded in facts, those who want to undermine it will likely not make much progress.

Summary

The Wrap-up section is a series of tables that cross-reference the decision paper scope, objectives, and issues to the actual work conducted and the recommendation. No new information is produced. The Wrap-up section is not a summary of the paper.

Appendices

When to Use Appendices

Appendices are important items that need not be in the body of the document. A good rule of thumb to determine if something goes in an Appendix rather than the body of the document is to ask: This information is important, but will I still get the full story without this detail? If the answer is yes, then it belongs in an Appendix.

Some examples of typical decision paper appendices:

- List of Participants. This is a list of the names and titles of those who participated in the development of the Decision Paper. You can segment the list in logical ways: core team, approvers, interviewees, auditors, etc. The benefit of this List of Participants appendix is that it helps to quell concern that the right people and departments were not involved or were not sufficiently involved. It can also include a RACI table to clarify the roles of each participant. (See the Missing Sections discussion in this guide.)

- Financial Tables. It is often a good idea not to weigh down the Alternatives and Recommendation section with detailed financial tables about their costs (one-time and ongoing) and benefits. These can be easily placed in an appendix, accessible to the inquisitive reader.

- Governance Meeting Schedule. This is a table listing all of the governance meetings. The primary purpose of having a Governance Meeting Schedule is to reinforce regular participation and guidance from the appropriate organizational leaders. Without this, some people, with no facts to support the assumption, will think the Decision Paper Ad Hoc team developed their work without input from leadership. You may expand this table to include key decisions made at each meeting.

- Detailed Tables. These are the full versions of any tables that appear in a summarized form in the body of the decision paper.

The Management Summary

How to Write the Management Summary

Once your decision paper is completely drafted, it will need to be summarized for the purpose of presenting it in a condensed form. This usually involves taking a document that is in long form—often written with Microsoft Word—and summarizing it into presentation form—often developed with Microsoft PowerPoint.

Unlike the story you built in your decision paper, which logically proceeds and builds up to the recommendation near the end, a Management Summary requires that you bow a bit to the journalism tactic of having the major message up front. That is also known as *Don't bury the lede.* Given the great range of topics (i.e., scopes) covered by decision papers, there are just a few pointers I would recommend when developing the Management Summary.

- Yes, Have a Management Summary. Sometimes there is no explicit ask that you develop a Management Summary. I recommend you develop a Management Summary regardless of whether it is requested. There will be many opportunities to put it to good use.

- Reusable. Create your Management Summary with the notion that it will be used again and again in various ways and settings to communicate a summary of the decision paper. Consider how, for example, the Management Summary of the Strategy to Close the Lollipop Division may be re-used to brief two newly elected members of the Board of Directors. Rather than scramble to assemble a summary for these Board Members, it would be better to invest no new time by just reusing the Management Summary.

- Executive Summary. Start the Management Summary with a one-page Executive summary. Depending on the intricacy and complexity of the scope of your decision paper, this can seem like quite a challenge. Nonetheless, I have found there is no better way to start the summary discussion than with a one-page synopsis of the entire story. Usually you will draw on the following sections of the complete decision paper to create the one-page summary: The Need, Findings, and the Recommendation part of Alternatives and Recommendation. Your one-page Executive summary gets to these points quickly: What is the need? What did you find out? What do you recommend?

- <u>Don't Cram In All the Details</u>. You will not be able to, nor should you try to include all the points (even all the major points) that are included in the decision paper. This is a pitfall that results in ludicrous situations such as having a 50-page decision paper *summarized* in a 40-page Management Summary.

- <u>Not a Substitute for Reading the Decision Paper</u>. Make clear to your audiences that reviewing and understanding the Management Summary cannot be viewed as a substitute for reading and understanding the decision paper. You want to be spared from situations where audiences will claim they were blindsided because interesting and provocative details were not in the Management Summary but were "buried" in the decision paper.

- <u>Consistent Terminology</u>. Keep terminology 100% consistent between the decision paper and the Management Summary. Period. If you don't, you will unnecessarily confuse your audience. See also the note on Consistent Terminology in Part 2 of this guide.

- <u>Don't Skirt Controversy</u>. Most decision papers have content that will be viewed as controversial. Recall our discussion that decision papers usually identify winners and losers. That is not because doing so is a goal; it just naturally comes about when completing the story of the decision paper. It is best to face this controversy up front in the Management Summary if it is relevant to the summarized story.

- <u>Presenting</u>. Most decision paper Management Summaries are presented to governance bodies, oversight bodies, constituents, stakeholders, rights holders, etc. Presenting is an involved topic area that is not covered in this guide. Just one piece of advice: leave plenty of time for dialogue. If you think it will take you an hour to cover the content of the Management Summary, schedule the meeting for two hours.

- <u>Prepare Last, Present First</u>. You will notice that this guide recommends you develop the Management Summary after the decision paper is completely drafted. There is no other way to ensure that the entirety of the analysis is fairly summarized. However, the Management Summary may be formally presented before the final decision paper is formally presented. While this is not entirely necessary, presenting the Management Summary first can help the various audiences better comprehend the details in the longer paper.

"Missing" Sections: Why Other Commonly Used Sections are Not Included

Many organizations likely have other sections in their standard decision paper format that are not included here. So that you don't think I somehow forgot them, below is my rationale for not having some commonly included decision paper sections in the standard proposed outline:

- Benefits. Time, money, and effort expended in the process of developing a decision paper must have some benefits. In business environments, the concept of achieving benefits can be a strong cultural force. Nonprofits, for example, exist to provide beneficial services in their areas of focus. However, I find segregating benefits in its own section causes them to be disjointed from the story of the decision paper. The outline I propose primarily embeds benefits in the Objectives section. Benefits-to-be-attained are defined as Objectives, often at the level of Business Objectives. But they can also logically be found at the System and Initiative Objectives levels, too. Sometimes benefits can also be found in the Methodology section. This makes sense, as you will make use of methods, practices, and tools that are beneficial to the organization.

- Key Deliverables. The alternatives will indeed have some key deliverables. If it is helpful to call those out, I recommend they be included in the Alternatives and Recommendation section. This way they are integrated into the story of the decision paper. The reader sees the deliverables in the context of the alternatives and recommended alternative.

- Major Milestones. It is often useful to have a schedule of major milestones in each proposed alternative. Include them with the Alternatives and Recommendation section, rather than in a separate section.

- Financials. Financials should be included in the Alternatives and Recommendation section. I advise keeping them as high-level as possible given the governing processes in your organization. The reason for that is efficiency: there is no need to expend a great deal of time and effort without knowing for sure if the recommended alternative will be supported. Define financial costs and financial benefits for one-time work and for ongoing (likely annual) operations.

- Responsibility Matrix / Organization. It may be helpful to show the organization (teams, positions, reporting relationships) of those involved in the decision paper and of those who will act on the alternatives. If this is helpful, include this information in the Methodology section for the organization preparing the decision paper (means) and in the Alternatives and Recommendation section for those executing the alternatives (ends).

- Success Metrics. Sometimes these are called Key Performance Indicators. Success metrics should be included in the Objectives section.

- Approvals. This is usually a very short section noting the name, title, and date for each individual who approved the decision paper. This should be included if it is part of your organization's standard. I would typically show this as an appendix or as the very last section in the body of the paper. I have not included it in the standard recommended outline, as I view it as extraneous to the paper itself.

- Voice of the Customer. Some decision papers have a Voice of the Customer (or similar wording) section to describe what the organization's customers may be experiencing and what they are expecting. Giving prominence to the views and interests of the customer is part of many organizations' culture and ethos. A Voice of the Customer section could indeed be important and relevant to the story of the decision paper. If it is, I recommend it be included in the Need section. Keeping the customer top of mind when conducting a decision paper exercise fits well with the basic *need* to take on that work.

- Guiding Principles. Guiding Principles are closely held beliefs that are major considerations when an organization makes decisions, makes judgments, or considers taking actions. They equate well to an individual's values. Some organizations refer to what might be called "Guiding Principles" as "company values." I recommend that such Guiding Principles be included in the sections where they are relevant. Usually, organization-wide Guiding Principles that holistically affect the decision paper are included in the Background section. They may also be included in the Objectives section prior to the delineation of the objectives. If the organization's Guiding Principles are solely about investment decisions, then they can be placed at the beginning of the Alternatives and Recommendation section. The organization that owns the Rivertown Plant might have a guiding principle with regard to its employees: Employee safety is our number one priority. This may well be placed in the Background section, as it applies to all aspects of the decision paper.

- <u>Lessons Learned</u>. Lessons Learned are embedded in the Findings, Analysis, and Conclusions sections. Some organizations split Lessons Learned in two, with titles such as What Went Well and What Needs Improvement. If this is the standard in your organization, the Lessons Learned language in Findings, Analysis, and Conclusions can be so structured.

- <u>Overview</u>. This is what I call the Management Summary section.

- <u>RACI Table</u>. RACI stands for Responsible, Accountable, Consulted, and Informed. For a decision paper, a RACI table would have the 15 sections of the decision paper as the y-axis, and roles and teams as the x-axis. This, for example, would make very clear the roles of the CEO, DPAH Team, Internal Audit, Outside Regulators, etc. Each cell would be populated with R, A, C, or I. RACI tables can be useful. If they are included, I would recommend they be included as an Appendix since they do not contribute to the building of the story of the decision paper.

- <u>Requirements</u>. Requirements are covered in the Scope section in the discussion of the scope of the end products. They may also be covered by items in the Need and Objectives sections. If it suits the subject of your decision paper, have a subsection in the Scope section called "Requirements."

- <u>Summary Conclusion</u>. Some organizations may have a standard requiring a Summary Conclusion section. This would be at the end of the document and provide a summary of key findings, key recommendations, takeaways, and actions. I do not recommend such a section, even though there is some value to reiterating the gist of the paper in one concluding section. Instead, I would point the reader to the Management Summary and the carefully structured entire contents of the decision paper. A good way to test the completeness of the Management Summary is to review it, knowing there is no other summary in the document.

- Call to Action. Some organizations have a Call to Action section in the paper that clearly and directly identifies the steps to be taken. Clear next steps are important. I recommend they be included in the Alternatives and Recommendation section. The actions to act on the recommendation are inseparable from the recommendation itself. If they are separated into two sections, some readers may agree to the recommendation in principle but disagree with the action steps. Also, any urgently needed actions should be so noted in the recommendation.

- Abstract. This is just another term for what I call the Management Summary, which is already included in the standard table of contents.

- Needs Assessment. This is the Need section.

Final Approval

Seeking Final Approval

My guidance here is very simple. Seek to have your decision paper ultimately approved at the highest level in the organization. In corporate structures, this would mean the CEO and perhaps even the Board of Directors. When the decision paper is subject to review and approval at lower organizational levels, a few dysfunctions are often evident:

- The individual or individuals tasked with reviewing and approving the decision paper may feel the need to preview it with the CEO (or CEO equivalent) on their own. This often results in complex and interesting decision papers being presented to the CEO without anyone on the decision paper development team present. This can lead to the rejection of the paper before it is published and without a chance for the development team to (logically) argue its analysis and conclusions.

- Despite any formal delegation of authority to the managers reviewing and approving (or not) the decision paper, they may not fully embrace this governance role. Consider how, for example, the decision papers we have used as examples—Rivertown Plant Explosion and Failed Financial Systems Project, for example—are likely to result in far-reaching changes in policy. The managers delegated responsibility for review and approval of the decision paper may back off by just stating policy changes must be made at the Board level.

If you try and cannot get review and approval at the highest level, then do all you can to formally present the decision paper to the highest levels. Do this with the approvers in the room. This has the de facto result of obtaining the okay of the most senior levels without breaking the decision paper governance structure.

Lack of Consensus

It is possible that the DPAH team will reach the end of their work and be split as a group as to key aspects of the report's recommendations. What to do, for example, if in the Seattle Office Closing decision paper case, a faction supports a recommendation to never have satellite offices again, versus a plurality of the members that fully support the creation of new offices but to stricter policy and planning standards?

The simple solution in this case is also the right solution. I have advised in the guide to have just one recommendation. However, if trying to achieve consensus fails, document both recommendations noting, *by name*, who supports the respective recommendations. Decision papers are ultimately products to be weighed, considered, and supported or not supported by senior leadership. In the case of Lack of Consensus, I advise not over-thinking it and just going with the split viewpoints in the final report. Executive and senior management will need to decide what recommendations to action and implement.

One concern I have here is that any approach that calls for prolonged dialogue to reach consensus will quickly turn into analysis paralysis—resulting in a failed decision paper effort.

Political Misapplications

At this late stage of the decision paper development process, the primary political games to watch out for have to do with delays and obstruction. Those not in favor of the decision paper's findings and recommendations may ask for more time, saying, "What's the rush?" This approach is highly effective in consensus-driven cultures. It is the primary reason I advise setting a firm timetable at the beginning of the decision paper development initiative.

Also be aware that some individuals are controlling by nature. They may seek to dominate or exert control over the review iterations. This must be dealt with by means of effective leadership and facilitation.

PART 2

The ABCs of Writing a Decision Paper

In this part of the guide, I will cover an array of other topics that are important but are not related to just one section of the decision paper. They are listed in alphabetical order.

Acronyms, Initialisms, Abbreviations

Using shortcuts to avoid long phrases and terms is a normal part of language. We hear them every day, and you will certainly want to use them in your decision paper. However, you will need to proceed with caution and awareness, or your use of acronyms, initialisms and abbreviations may create reader confusion.

A quick summary of what these terms mean:

- **Acronyms** are formed typically by the first letters of a multi-word term. They create a term that is pronounced as a single word. For example, in the United States, OSHA stands for Occupational Health and Safety Administration, and everyone in manufacturing pronounces it "OH-sha."

- **Initialisms** are a type of acronym. They are also typically formed by the first letters of a multi-word term, but initialism is not pronounced as if it were a single word. They are referred to by their initial letters. There are many common examples, including YMCA, ATM, and SAT. Hybrid initialisms exist as well, such as JPEG and CD-ROM.

- **Abbreviations** are simply the shortening of a long term or set of terms to communicate efficiently. For example, we type *etc.* rather than *et cetera.*

It may be, for example, that the Rivertown Plant Explosion follow-up requires a great deal of involvement from the government's Ministry of Industrial and Technical Safety. If your decision paper refers to it 20 or 30 times, that's a long phrase to continually use. If the common term is MITS and everyone pronounces it like "mitts," then by all means use MITS. But you will need to introduce the term the first time you use it.

I also recommend repeating the terms in the body of the decision paper if there is a large gap between when the term was introduced and the section that includes it. In other words, someone who reads a term defined on page 3 and then sees it again for the first time on page 47 is unlikely to remember what it stands for.

Adjectives

In decision papers, use adjectives to describe; do not use adjectives to interpret. Adjectives will help you to better describe facts and evidence. If the Safety Operations Manual at the Rivertown Plant was recently updated, it's okay to say "the recently updated Safety Operations Manual." But it is not okay to say "the recently updated and likely flawed Safety Operations Manual." If you have a finding that the Safety Operations Manual was incomplete, difficult for employees to find, difficult to understand, and contained obsolete safety practices, then say that explicitly in the Findings section of the decision paper. Likewise, adjectives should not be used to make snide, unprofessional commentary. So, don't say, "The allegedly qualified business strategy team at headquarters did not foresee the large drop in the Lollipop Division's profitability."

Anecdotes

Anecdotes are one-off stories very likely to be firmly based on facts, but they can be erroneously presented as proof of a pervasive problem or trend. Sharing such stories as part of fact-finding for a decision paper is fine. The warning is to be careful that a one-off anecdote does not get misrepresented as a trend or theme. In other words, any trend can be extrapolated from one data point. It would be a mistake to do so.

Auditable

The entire decision paper development and presentation process should be well documented in case the work is audited. Sometimes the audit comes well after the completion of the paper, so the documentation should be understandable even if a member of the team is not present. For example, formal interview write-ups and documentation reviews are important working papers that should be retained and indexed in case of an audit. You would likely never want to include such detail in the body of the decision paper. But, if they are closely examined by an auditor, the working papers should synch up perfectly with the content of the final decision paper.

Having all documentation and notes well organized for a later review goes beyond readiness for an audit. For example, a potential investor or acquirer may want someone on their team to review working notes as part of their due diligence. That is not an audit, but it still requires documents to be organized, complete and auditable.

Communications Plan

A decision paper development effort should have an explicit Communications (or "Comms") Plan. This should be produced early in the process, be developed with the assistance of a Communications professional, and be regularly maintained and updated. It would include strategy and plan for communicating with all constituent groups, stakeholders, and rights holders. Depending on the subject of the decision paper, the constituents can include external groups such as the public, media, labor unions, shareholders, and regulators. The Comms Plan should consider and plan for communications during startup, ongoing progress, and wrap-up stages of the decision paper development.

Consistency of Terminology

Use consistent terminology—always. This is a very simple rule to follow and will go a long way to making your decision paper clearer. Many if not most of the readers of your decision paper will not be intimately familiar with the organizations and teams referred to in the paper. Likewise, many of the readers will not be familiar with the policies, practices, standards, etc. that are perhaps part of normal operations. There is a simple way to help your reader with this lack of familiarity: always use consistent terms. Do not change terminology during the course of the paper. For example, if you need to refer to the Project Management Policy, then always refer to it as the "Project Management Policy." Don't change the wording so that the same document is referred to as the "PMO's Policy" without any reason or without any heads-up to the reader.

Courage

Writing decision papers on topics of great consequence (the point of this guide) is not for the faint of heart. You must demonstrate courage. Courage does not mean you don't become sensitive to your audience's reactions. Courage means you don't let fear stop you from taking the appropriate actions and saying what needs to be said.

Editing

James J. Kilpatrick, on the very first page of his work *The Writer's Art,* captures the essence of something important: "so much bad writing abounds."[10] I can't add to that. Considering that most people do not write clearly and succinctly, I am a strong advocate for using a professional editor to review decision papers. You can involve a professional editor during the early drafts, but certainly do so to review the final draft. Your editor needs to come from an uninvolved and independent source. This may mean bypassing editors on staff to go outside for independence. It is worth it. There is the added benefit that someone from the outside will be a good judge as to whether those not involved and those not familiar with the history of the decision paper topic can truly understand the *story* the decision paper lays out.

Elephants in the Room

Elephants in the room is a phrase used to refer to concerns or facts that are important to one's audience and/or constituents—regardless of whether they are recognized by those in authority. Such concerns have a powerful way of occupying people's attention. To not mention them would be like giving a presentation on a mundane subject while not pointing out there is an elephant standing in the back of the room. A real elephant would be large, smelly, and dangerous—not easy to ignore. This is why, for example, I advise an exception to the guidance that the Background section should proceed chronologically in cases

---

[10] James J. Kilpatrick, *The Writer's Art* (Kansas City and New York: Andrews, McMeel & Parker, 1984), 9.

where a big event is on everyone's minds, such as the fatalities that occurred at the Rivertown Plant. The fact of the fatalities is the elephant in the room that should be addressed first in the Background section.

You should be aware of the elephants in the room with regard to your decision paper subject and explicitly address them. Some decision paper authors balk at this when the elephant is fictitious or the result of FUD (fear, uncertainty, and doubt). For example, if there was a widely believed rumor that the Seattle office lost customers and opportunities because competitors wiretapped the building, the decision paper should address the rumor, even if it was quickly and easily proven to be false.

Exclamation Points and All Capital Letters

When should you use exclamation points in a decision paper? Quite simply: never. William Zinsser and Strunk and White, experts in non-fiction writing, advise that exclamation marks be used sparingly. Any emphasis you are working to achieve can be provided by means of wording alone. For example, the Rivertown Plant Explosion decision paper may very well include the sentence, "Loss of life in any of our facilities, for any reason, is unacceptable." This is a rather grave and somber matter, delivered soberly as a matter of fact. No exclamation point would improve this delivery.

My advice is the same for putting words in all capital letters: Don't do it. It gives the impression of emotional shouting. That is not the tenor you want to convey in a decision paper. The only words that should appear in all capitals are standard acronyms. Did you know that the musical group ABBA's name is in all capital letters because it is an anagram of the names of the four founders of the group? It's not because they are shouting.

Extending the Ad Hoc Team

The decision paper ad hoc (DPAH) team may gel as a team. The team members may come to enjoy their task of developing a decision paper, they may enjoy the visibility it gives them in the organization, and they may come to make it part of their identity as they work together to solve key problems for the organization. This is all good and desirable. But, if it leads to the DPAH group wanting to continue its existence past the finalization and approval of their decision paper, then it becomes dangerous. My primary concern with extending decision paper teams is that it flies in the face of the transition of the recommendations to ongoing functions. For example, the Failed Financial Systems Project will likely have recommendations for project governance. Those recommendations should be handed to the Project Management Office to implement, not shadow-managed by the DPAH team. Getting the PMO to own and execute such change will be an important step to mainstream the supported recommendations for lasting change.

My warning about extending the decision paper team is the primary reason I recommend the awkward term "ad hoc" be included in the name of the team charged with developing the decision paper. It makes it very clear that this team is for a specific purpose only and then will cease to exist.

Graphs, Tables, and Charts

If graphs, tables, or charts can clearly explain the messages you are presenting, then by all means include graphs, tables, or charts. Be careful not to force their usage, as some do almost as a quota. Notions such as "I try to have at least one graph every 5 pages" are not helpful if they do not give primacy to clearly showing data trends and contrasts.

Some pointers:

- <u>Two Dimensions</u>. In situations where there is some complexity to what needs to be explained yet the topic can be simplified in two dimensions—an x and a y axis in a graph, or columns and rows in a table—then having graphs or tables usually helps the reader understand. Consider, for example, a table for the Seattle Office decision paper that shows revenue for the three most recent fiscal years (the x-axis) split between Legacy Clients (clients for 5 years or more) and New Clients (clients for less than 5 years). The table's cells can show total revenue and percent of all revenue for that fiscal year. If the table shows a large total and percentage of revenue from Existing Clients, it brings into question the new Seattle office's success in attracting new clients.

- Powerful Distinctions. Laying data out in tables can call attention to significant disparities or contrasts in data. For example, suppose the Failed Financial Systems Project decision paper had a table showing software bugs by three types of software programming: commercial off-the-shelf without enhancement, commercial off-the-shelf with enhancement, and custom programming. If a large percentage of the bugs are in the custom programming category, this may be an enlightening indication that the software as purchased had a low rate of errors, but the team developing the customizations may have been the real source of the software quality problems.

- Trends. The presence or absence of a trend can be meaningful, and graphs are often the clearest way to show whether a trend exists. For example, the Rivertown Plant Explosion paper may show a multi-year trend of gradually decreasing employee injury incidents and employee time off due to on-the-job injuries up to the point of the accident. This can be clearly shown in a graph. Whether this finding is interesting will be analyzed in the Analysis section. The trend in the aforementioned example might support the notion that there was a successful safety culture in place at Rivertown and that this accident was more of an anomaly.

- Pie Charts. Pie charts are best used for data that shows a long list of characteristics of one heterogeneous data set. For example, a pie chart of lollipop sales per consumer age groupings might show a huge dependency on current sales on those 50 years and older, with very low sales to those 25 years or younger. This data could be very useful and interesting as an indication that the Lollipop Division was overly reliant on the older consumer segment, helping to explain the continual reduction in sales year-over-year.

- Process Flows. Where process flow (sometimes called workflow) is important for the reader to understand, you may include process flow diagrams. These show the flow of work from processing areas such as organizational departments, information systems, and outside services. Process flow diagramming is a broad topic not addressed in this guide, but I do have a couple of bits of advice on process flows:

  - Swim Lanes. Use the concept of *swim lanes*. This is where each organizational unit, in-house system, and service provider is shown in its own horizontal lane, and the process flow arrows bridge over the various lanes. It is easier for a reader to understand the flows when lanes are used to define who or what is doing each action.

- o One Direction. If possible, show the process flowing in one direction only, typically left to right. Arrows flowing back or recursing through the flow diagram can be very confusing for readers to follow.

- Colors. Having colors (i.e., hues other than black and white) in graphs, tables and charts can further improve comprehension of what you are communicating. When using colors, I would advise:

  - o Be consistent throughout the document as to what each color means. For example, it will confuse a reader if one graphic uses red to indicate a problem or missed target and another graphic uses red for the newest franchise locations.

  - o Define the meanings of colors with a legend. For example, don't leave it to the reader to guess if yellow is just highlighting or indicates some warning or miss.

  - o Be aware of how the colors will look when rendered in a black and white printout.

  - o When laying text over color graphics, ensure there is enough contrast to make the text readable. For example, it is hard for most people to read black letters that are printed over a deep blue color.

  - o Be aware that some readers will be colorblind, lacking some ability to distinguish between colors.

If you want a best practices reference for graphs and charts, look up some of Edward Tufte's work on visual display of quantitative information. Three titles I highly recommend are listed in the bibliography at the end of this guide. Otherwise, my advice is to keep graphics, charts, and tables simple and intuitively easy to understand.

Humor

I have already advised against trying to be funny when creating a title for your paper. The same goes for the entire decision paper document. Do not use humor, cute phrasing, or smart-alecky wording. At best, they will cheapen the entire document, make you look unserious, and distract readers from the message you are trying to communicate. At worst, they will be met with horror and incredulity commensurate with the gravity of the topic.

Let me emphasize: When I say "Do not use humor," I do not mean just in situations where lives have been lost, such as the Rivertown Plant Explosion, or jobs are being lost, as in the shutdown of the Lollipop Division. Every decision paper reflects a serious investment of effort and resources—often scarce resources. Respect that investment by taking your role seriously. Humor does not belong in decision papers.

"I" Language

I have often heard the recommendation that when writing in a business or formal organization context, one should never use the pronoun "I." This is really nonsense. The advice I give on this subject is to use "I" when it makes sense and "we" when it makes sense to factually convey who is taking the action implied by the verb in the sentence. You may have noticed that some writers go to great lengths to obscure the actors in their language. For example, you might see: "It has been determined that the historical quality problems with the accounting system merit investigation and perhaps investment." With this painful use of passive voice, you have no idea who did the determining. It would be clearer to say: "Rob Hastings, Head of Internal Audit, and I, as Head of Technology, determined that the historical quality problems . . ."

Remember, you are endeavoring to inform, not obscure. Write "I" where it is the simplest way to convey that it is you who is the source, you who is the actor. Use "we" when an action has multiple authors including yourself.

Inspire

"There are only three ways to generate human connection and conduct: You can coerce, motivate, or inspire."[11]. This is from Dov Seidman's book, *How: Why How We Do Anything Means Everything*. While you prepare your decision paper, keep this statement in mind. Ultimately you want to inspire the reader to buy into your story and support your recommendations because they make sense and will achieve the greater goals—not because their bosses tell them to, and not because of perils, chaos, and dismay. Inspire; don't create fear.

Length

This guide provides very little advice on the preferred length of a decision paper. That is intentional. Some sections of the standard decision paper are best kept brief, such as Wrap-up and Intended Audience, because their focus is narrow. Other sections, such as Background and Findings, may become very long. My advice on length is to mostly ignore it. The richness and seriousness of the topics discussed are what drives the length of the decision paper sections. In that respect, the document will be as long as it needs to be.

If you are asked why your decision paper is too long or too short, I advise you to reply that that question is not helpful. It's the wrong question. If some readers complain the document is too long, then you can direct them to read the Management Summary (which itself contains a shorter Executive summary) and then decide on their own if they want to read the rest of the document.

It is important to say what needs to be said without excessive repetition and without padding the document with details that are not relevant or helpful. If you consider how weighty and serious some of the subject areas of decision papers are, then there can be no blind advice about length. Include all the words that need to be stated.

---

[11] Dov Seidman, *How: Why How We Do Anything Means Everything* (Hoboken, New Jersey: John Wiley & Sons, 2007), xxv.

Mosquitoes

By *mosquitoes*, I mean pointless annoyances that provide no value and only disrupt and distract. I recommend DPAH teams introduce and openly discuss the concept of mosquitoes as a way to recognize them and swat them down. In short, mosquitos suck the blood out of you, are annoying pains, distract those who need to focus, and provide no value-add for the bother they introduce.

For example, a member of the DPAH may want to go on at length about how the Financial Systems project that failed would have been successful if only the prior CEO had not retired. This might be interesting and of value to discuss once. But discussing it ten times is just a valueless annoyance—a mosquito.

Printable

Your decision paper should be perfectly comprehensible and presentable both on screen and when printed. This means you must check how the document looks both on screen and in print before you distribute it. If the document is printed, then the margins, headings, graphics, etc. must print properly. Do not advise readers on whether to print the document or not. This is a personal choice—some readers prefer to read paper documents, others prefer to read on a screen.

Quotable

Construct your most important sentences so that they are quotable out of context. The power of this is best illustrated with examples.

This sentence is awkward to quote: "The largest local client was displeased and wrote to Board when informed of the closure plans."

This sentence says the same thing but is more quotable out of context: "Jose Smith, the CEO of the largest client in our Washington State / British Columbia market, Acme Northern Services, was displeased when informed of the plans to close the Seattle office; he wrote the Board to express his displeasure."

Another example comes from this decision paper guide:

This sentence is awkward to quote: "Such a section could indeed be important and relevant to the story of the decision paper."

It is more quotable to say: "A Voice of the Customer section could indeed be important and relevant to the story of the decision paper."

Both are equally understandable when reading the entire section. One is much clearer when quoted out of context.

You may wonder why quotability matters. The contents of a decision paper may be discussed and debated in various formal and informal settings. You can facilitate that discussion by making your content easier to quote with no loss of meaning.

Quoting

You will undoubtedly find the need to quote sources and source materials in your decision papers.

For quotes derived from documented sources, ensure you are quoting the correct version. I have seen decision paper authors get their hands on a pre-release draft of a document and quote it in the decision paper. Unless you state very clearly that the document you are quoting is a pre-release draft, such a practice is unacceptable. As the decision paper is finalized, it is useful to have someone check that all quotes from documented sources are accurate.

You may have reasons to include quotes derived from verbal discussions that lack official minutes or other documented records. This is fine, but to the extent possible, you should obtain documented support for the accuracy of the quote from the person you are quoting. Decision papers can lose a lot of credibility if someone comes forward and says they were misquoted.

That said, remember the advice in the Background section regarding "very bad facts." Accurate quotes that add genuine value to the decision paper should be included. There is no need to avoid using a quote just because it will make someone look bad.

Really Big Number Syndrome

If your decision paper recommends a large expenditure, you may have to deal with the irrational ways some people react to really big numbers—Really Big Number Syndrome. Sometimes big numbers trigger an overreaction; other times, they may lead to scope creep. For example, the Rivertown Plant Explosion decision paper might recommend demolishing the existing plant and opening a new "greenfield" plant. The cost for this would likely be in the billions of dollars. Some stakeholders may assert that the cost cannot possibly be borne, failing to understand the full context of the expenditure, such as what will happen if the money is *not* spent. Other stakeholders will say things like, "If we are spending $3.5 billion, then I am sure we can include a bowling alley and pickleball courts for employees R and R." The fact that a very large budget number is proposed does not mean that scope control is abandoned.

It is important to anticipate both varieties of reactions when large numbers are under discussion. The tools you need to manage Really Big Number Syndrome are readily at hand: use the decision paper's documented scope and objectives to address any concerns regarding the degree of investment and whether it is appropriate.

Reviewing Drafts

As I briefly summarized in the introduction, decision papers are developed in the context of a governance structure. Sometimes, governance is provided by the executive leadership team at their regular meetings. Other times, special governance structures (i.e., task forces) are established. Special task forces can be effective governance for decision paper development, but one must be aware that such committees can get dysfunctional.

As the decision paper is under development, you will need to decide whether to share drafts with key constituents, stakeholders, and rights holders. Decision papers that are developed in some guise of secrecy and then presented in full form are often rejected immediately. Key constituents would have no sense of ownership if they were kept away from adding their perspective and advice as the key parts of the paper take shape. On the whole, I think it is helpful to do so, but here are some benefits and drawbacks:

- Benefits:
  - <u>Value-added Input</u>. Knowledgeable constituents, stakeholders, and rights holders may provide advice that ends up being of great value to the decision paper developers. I have seen this happen many times.

  - <u>Sense Of Ownership</u>. Allowing and fully embracing participation by those not directly tasked with creating the decision paper facilitates their sense of ownership and a genuine spirit of teamwork.

  - <u>The Principle Of "No Surprises</u>." Regardless of whether individuals agree with the final outcome, they cannot use the pretense of being surprised as a way to reject or diminish the outcome.

- Drawbacks:
  - <u>Participant Confusion</u>. Some participants may become confused as to how decision paper governance works. Such participants might think that the development of a decision paper is a democratic exercise where all get to vote—or perhaps even exercise veto authority—on even the smallest details. When presenting drafts for review, make it clear to participants that not all input will be used, simply because complete consensus is rarely achievable, nor would it be compatible with effective oversight.

  - <u>Comments On Style And Format</u>. Some participants will provide input on the style and format of the decision paper rather than on its substance. This is where it helps to have standards for decision paper content—such as those presented in this guide. State clearly that you are soliciting input on the paper's content, not its appearance or the perfection of its grammar and spelling. Emphasize that professional editors will review the final document for style, spelling, grammar, and format.

Stupidity

The existence of *stupidity* is real – it is part of the context in which most decision papers are developed. Please try not to reject the notion because considering it may be offensive to you. If you want your work to spur progress, solve problems, and bring opportunities within reach, you will need to know how to deal with stupidity.

Dietrich Bonhoeffer explored the subject of stupidity about 80 years ago in his *Letters and Papers from Prison.* [12] He wrote, "Neither protests nor the use of force accomplish anything [against stupidity]; reasons fall on deaf ears; facts that contradict one's prejudgment simply need not be believed [. . .] and when facts are irrefutable they are just pushed aside as inconsequential." Indeed, dealing with stupidity is a formidable challenge.

It would be wise not to confuse stupidity with ignorance (in its classic definition) or lies. Ignorance is merely not knowing. Why are some European competitors seemingly more successful with their lollipop sales? I don't know. That is something I am ignorant about.

Lies are a class by themselves affiliated with manipulation. To lie deliberately has nothing to do with being stupid. Those are independent concepts. However, some lies are directed to the stupid in recognition that the stupid will believe some lies when they view favorably the source of the lies from a perspective of appearance or affiliation.

Stupid people are not thinking clearly. In some ways they are not thinking clearly deliberately. It is therefore not just difficult to get them to see and accept reason, it is often completely impossible. The more you try to convince the stupid to follow a logical path that does not lead to what their preconceived notions tell them is the right answer, the more they distrust the source of the pleas for logic.

Sometimes those with cogent thinking but less than pure motives will take advantage of the stupid to serve their own interests. They could be thinking: *Why not support and foster an environment of lack of thought if it helps me?*

---

[12] Dietrich Bonhoeffer, *Letters and Papers from Prison* (Minneapolis, Minnesota: Fortress Press, 2015), 9–12.

Many of the people you work with and interact with do not engage with logic and reasoning but instead use emotion or biases as nonthinking shortcuts to viewpoints and conclusions. They start with an outcome, then build the logic steps back from there. This is stupidity in action. In some organizational cultures, this type of behavior is tolerated and maybe even encouraged. It is at times encouraged when the nonthinking behavior is part of unquestioning obedience to authority. It is very challenging to develop and present a decision paper that is based on reason in such an environment.

People who lack a logical progression to their thinking and who draw conclusions based on unfounded assumptions, incorrect "facts" or gut feel will likely be in your sphere of constituents, stakeholders, and rights holders. When you put them in a room (virtual or not) to discuss an important issue or problem, they will meander from subject to subject unless a skilled facilitator directs them to stay on topic. They may spend large amounts of time on minor issues whose allure is not their relevance to the topic but something inane, such as how important the issue was on another, very different initiative.

To counteract the world of the stupids, I recommend two approaches:

- Your decision paper must be logical and directed toward genuinely reasonable priorities. Don't compromise the logical integrity of the decision paper. The Decision Paper Ad Hoc (DPAH) team leaders must use their facilitation skills to dismiss seductive but ultimately meaningless diversions. This can best be done in workshop settings where the reasoning and unreasoning people are both in attendance. There is no reason to call participants stupid in such a setting; however, it is important to deal with their illogic head-on.

- Alas, it is the nature of stupidity that some people stubbornly embrace it, to the point that no amount of logic or reasoning will suffice to get the stupids to think clearly. It is a wise insight when Bonhoeffer says, "Against stupidity we are defenseless."[13] In that case, while it is not ideal, it is important to amass enough allies to support the logical analysis and conclusions of the decision paper, despite what the stupids are saying. In more casual words:

---

[13] Bonhoeffer, *Letters and Papers from Prison*, 9.

The stupid people need to be carried to the finish line. The decision paper authors need enough allies to make that happen.

In sum, stupidity exists, and writers of decision papers must be ready to deal with it in a dispassionate yet firm manner so that an effective decision paper development process can proceed.

Thinking

One way to look at a decision paper is that it is literally a thought piece—it is a thorough elucidation of logical thinking, stepping through the subject scope soundly, ultimately reaching a recommendation.

Much has been written about avoiding logical fallacies. There are long lists of various fallacies to be avoided. Serious writers of business decision papers should have a working understanding of logical fallacies so they can identify them when they appear and quash them before they cause damage to the decision paper development process. I recommend the book *Thinking 101* by Professor Woo-Kyoung Ahn. Professor Ahn, in my opinion, takes a more positive view of the subject than most. She focuses on how to "reason better" by embracing "actionable strategies" to improve reasoning (i.e., thinking) and by being cognizant of and therefore on guard for common ways people engage in flawed logic.[14]

While the subject of logical fallacies and Professor Ahn's book cover vast topics, I will highlight one that is of particular importance to the development of business decision papers: confirmation bias. Professor Ahn identifies confirmation bias as the worst of all of the cognitive biases.[15] Confirmation bias is "our tendency to confirm what we already believe."[16] This creates the illusion of a valuable shortcut through the decision paper process. Deriders would say, "We already know the answer; why are we wasting everyone's time with a decision paper?" Overcoming confirmation bias can be particularly difficult in cultures that embrace it as part of their identity of being *action-oriented*. The fundamental danger here is that confirmation bias can and often does stop

---

[14] Woo-Kyoung Ahn, *Thinking 101: Why We So Often Get Things Wrong in Life and How We Can All Do Better* (New York: Flatiron Books, 2022), 5.

[15] Ahn, *Thinking 101*, 58.

[16] Ahn, *Thinking 101*, 43.

the identification of relevant facts, actual root causes, and best paths forward. The illusion of action takes over where the emphasis should be on doing what makes the most sense.

If you are not yet convinced of the danger confirmation bias presents to decision paper development, consider the "not me" bias—the belief that while others may have certain biases, we ourselves are immune.[17] The blind overconfidence otherwise smart people will display can be understood as the combination of not-me and confirmation biases. People with this bias risk subverting the development of quality—and therefore useful—decision papers. Beware and be on guard.

Tone

Achieving the right tone in the writing of a decision paper is a bit hard to describe.

Be relaxed, professional, and clear. Convey your message as if you were doing it verbally in a formal setting, always following the rules of standard written English.

Do not be angry, defensive, argumentative, sarcastic, snide, snarky, excitable, superior, condescending, bombastic, or overly formal. These tones will alienate your readers and are never necessary.

Word choices are part of what makes hitting the right tone difficult. You want to use the right words to describe, as well as you can, the content of each decision paper section. Some readers, however, may perceive a bit of condescension if some words are long or obscure. But do not sacrifice the clarity of your message in an attempt to achieve accessibility. My advice is to err on the side of using the right words to capture exactly what you want to convey. For example, in the Failed Financial Systems Project decision paper, if the best word to describe the high quality and completeness of a comprehensive software testing program—one composed of skilled people using proven methods, templates, tools, and standards—is *gestalt*, then use that term.

Overall, your tone should have an element of *seriousness* to it. The paper

---

[17] Ahn, *Thinking 101*, 8.

you are writing is on an important and consequential topic. The tone throughout the document should convey that the authors understand and respect that seriousness.

Tyranny of the Articulate

Some people—either decision paper ad hoc (DPAH) team members or involved constituents, stakeholders, or rights holders—may be very vocal. It is the rare organization that does not have some individuals who seem to always dominate the conversation and/or question so many things that it seems to all that progress will never be made. These individuals, by the way they interrupt and dominate, will prevent those who are timid or lack confidence from offering comments even when they want to. This is the tyranny of the articulate.

As a preparer of decision papers, it is important that you not allow any person, group, or faction so much floor time that they effectively silence the views of others. This is another reason I take the view that the leaders of the DPAH should have very good facilitation skills. These skills are crucial for ensuring that no one group or individual dominates the conversation.

Uncertainty

Dealing with uncertainty is inherent in the entire process of creating and acting on a decision paper. Decision papers involve encountering, researching and analyzing facts and events, and they culminate in alternatives and a recommendation. Uncertainties will be encountered multiple times along the journey to a recommendation. Until this work is addressed in the process of developing the decision paper, all those involved need to be okay with uncertainty.

There is great risk to the integrity of the decision paper process, and therefore to the validity of the analysis and the soundness of the recommendations, when uncertainty is viewed as a problem rather than the natural condition that it is. In some organizational cultures, it is not possible to enter into discussions of great consequence to the organization and admit that there is uncertainty about events, facts, causes and remedies. In such organizations, admitting uncertainty can be viewed as a weakness and even intolerable.

In reality, accepting uncertainty is a key to nimble learning and adaptation. For further information on this subject, one can read *Uncertain: The Wisdom and Wonder of Being Unsure* by Maggie Jackson.[18]

Vendors and Service Providers

I would be remiss not to include some guidance on dealing with vendors and service providers—in other words, dealing with entities that are part of the story but over which you and your governance process may have only limited influence. My primary advice is to draw no distinctions between vendor and non-vendor when developing all sections of the decision paper. Pursue and involve all entities as needed. There may be need for special arrangements with vendors, such as new contracts to get vendor time and responses. That is merely a logistical consideration. But I would avoid artificial constraints or limitations. For example, if it makes sense to interview the entire 6-person team that developed the latest Lollipop Division strategy, then do that. It would be silly to say that only employee team members will be interviewed if one or more contractors played a key role in developing the strategy.

It is important not to be naive regarding the loyalties of vendors. Typically, vendors will feel their primary allegiance is to their own organization. DPAH teams that are working on problems and understanding root causes need to be particularly wary. This does not mean you should exclude vendors, but you should take a more critical view of their input if their primary focus appears to be on keeping themselves and their organization blameless.

Zinsser on Writing

A decision paper is written with a point. The writing style you adopt will either help the reader get your points or get in the way. For the last

---

[18] Maggie Jackson, *Uncertain: The Wisdom and Wonder of Being Unsure* (Lanham, Maryland: Rowman & Littlefield Publishing Group, 2023).

entry (alphabetically) on the ABCs of writing a decision paper, I turn to William Zinsser.

If you have read all the way to this point, you may have noticed that I frequently reference *On Writing Well*, William Zinsser's best-selling and classic guide for writing nonfiction. The book includes a chapter on business writing. His guidance on writing style is an excellent summation of the style I advise for decision papers. Among his guidelines:

> {My] four articles of faith [are] clarity, simplicity, brevity, and humanity.

> Almost any subject can be made accessible in good English.

> If what you write is ornate, or pompous, or fuzzy, that's how you'll be perceived.

> If you work for an institution, whatever your job, whatever your level, be yourself when you write. You will stand out as a real person among the robots.[19]

And one final word of advice from Mr. Zinsser comes from his book *Writing to Learn*: "The essence of writing is rewriting."[20] Iterate through your decision paper document enough times to make sure it has integrity and makes sense as a whole.

---

[19] Zinsser, *On Writing Well*, 171–177.

[20] William Zinsser, *Writing to Learn* (New York: Harper & Row, 1988), 15.

PART 3
Now What?

I am going to presume that you have read this guide up to this point. You have been presented with a standard format for decision papers, a lot of advice on how to develop the decision paper content, and some advice on how to deal with political interference from bad political actors. "Now what?" you may ask.

Many of you work at organizations that rely heavily on analysis, collaboration, and thinking to arrive at strategic decisions regarding investment, organization, business focus, and, perhaps most importantly, problem-solving. In other words, your organization has a lot riding on having a sound, complete, and honest decision paper process.

If you are serious about how your organization develops decision papers and are game to give my guidance a serious chance, then you will need a project to roll out the standards and recommendations described in this guide. This rollout program should include:

- A plan to create decision paper content and governance standards for the organization—or to revise existing standards, if any. Please read the copyright page of this book and include the following attribution in your new or revised standards guide:

    Material from *Writing Business Decision Papers: A Comprehensive How-To Guide* © 2024 Erwin Martinez has been incorporated into this internal policy manual with the permission of the copyright owner.

- A communications plan that includes a presentation to senior leadership in your organization as to the changes that will be made to decision paper standards, processes, and governance.

- An analysis of changes to existing policies and committee terms of reference, and implementation of required changes.

- A real-life demonstration paper to pilot the process. I recommend a substantial, important subject area for the demonstration. You cannot prove the effectiveness of this new approach in a low-priority or overly simple example. Detractors may point that out and pretend the new approach will only work for simple, low-priority change.

I recommend implementing the full set of recommendations in this guide to start. Then (of course) embark on a process of continuous improvement, during which you can customize and enhance if needed. There is a reason why I advise against selecting some of the recommendations in this guide but not others. As a general rule, a good way to ensure failure when implementing strategic changes is to selectively make changes in some areas and not others. Fixing a chair with four broken legs will not work if you decide to just fix three of the legs and see how it goes. Go all in, or don't go.

If your organization has a natural home for decision paper standards, then I recommend that it continues. For example, if the Enterprise Project Management Office (EPMO) in your organization owns decision paper and business case standards, there is no need to change that in order to follow the recommendations in this guide.

One final thought about political misapplications: Critics will question your motives as you embark on improving the decision paper process in your organization. More than that, they will claim that updating the decision paper process is just a guise to achieve some agenda that you've had all along. Critics will couch their attempts to prevent change with questions like "But you don't really know?" and "Isn't all this for the CEO to decide and not you?" Use the entirety of this guide to deal with such criticism. I wrote it with that use in mind.

A sample decision paper outline follows this chapter. Use it, the glossary, and the bibliography as you move forward. I wish you success.

Appendix
The Santa Claus Decision Paper, Selected Sections

- Findings
  - Noted children behavior metrics. Measurements include no time-outs, 100% brushing teeth twice a day, cleanliness of bedrooms, no fights among siblings.
  - The night before, the children left cookies and grass out for Santa and the reindeer to have a snack.
  - In the morning:
    - Presents were in evidence; they were not there the night before
    - Cookies were no longer there, but there were some crumbs
    - Grass was no longer there, but a few strands of it were nearby
    - Soot stains were in evidence near the fireplace that were not there before
- Analysis
  - The existence of presents is consistent with the tradition that Santa rewards good children with presents.
  - Disappearance of cookies and grass, state of plate with crumbs, and state of floor with pieces of grass are consistent with Santa and the reindeer having eaten the snacks.
  - Appearance of soot stains indicates the chimney was disturbed, consistent with one or more beings (persons and/or reindeer) having climbed down and up the chimney.
- Conclusion
  - Using deductive reasoning and the indications of the evidence:

While the children were sleeping, Santa and reindeer visited the house, gained access through the chimney, and rewarded the children with gifts for being good. While this cannot be proven conclusively, it is a reasonable conclusion given the findings and analysis.

- Alternatives

  - Option 1. Children continue to be good for yet another year, with the expectation of Santa again rewarding them with gifts on Christmas morning.

  - Option 2. Consider that the causal relationship between being good and getting presents was not verified and perhaps was just a coincidence. Children do not need to be good this year and can act up and be annoying imps if they so choose.

- Recommendation: Option 1. Reasoning is that there are other benefits to the children behaving well for the year, and there is sufficient evidence (but not proof) of the causal relationship between being good and Santa visiting the house and providing presents.

Glossary

Assumptions. Statements that are considered true for planning purposes and are clearly documented. These may be better termed "working assumptions" in that the work to prepare the decision paper and/or execute the recommendations of the decision paper will proceed without hesitation as if the assumptions were true.

Business Objectives. The net effect of the end products, but not the end products themselves. The ultimate purpose of the decision paper.

Constraints. Limitations on the possible work, findings, analyses, and recommendations. Constraints have the characteristic of being insurmountable.

Decision Paper. A single document that lays out a logical journey to address a defined scope involving an identified problem or opportunity of great importance to an organization. A decision paper often includes a recommendation for action that addresses all aspects of the scope. It may, alternatively, make a bold recommendation to take no action.

Dependencies. Tasks, actions, and decisions that must be made *before* the finalization of the decision paper (Means) or before the execution of recommendations (Ends). Just like Constraints, Dependencies have the characteristic of being insurmountable.

Ends. The output, irrespective of the means. In the context of decision papers, this is the work that comes *after* the decision paper's recommendation is approved, funded, and supported.

Facilitation. Guiding and working with a diverse group of individuals to proceed productively, creatively, and thoughtfully. Includes quashing disruptions and distractions that hinder a productive, creative, and thoughtful process.

Goal. An overarching target that is achieved through the completion of one or often many discrete objectives.

Governance. Guidance, direction, and endorsement.

Guiding Principles. The closely held beliefs that are major considerations when an organization makes decisions or judgments or considers taking actions. They equate well to an individual's values. Some organizations call them *company values.*

Initiative Objectives. The required characteristics of the initiative, irrespective of what is being implemented. Typically, these are in the realm of working within a timeframe or with a limit on resources (budget, people and material). Sometimes used to mean the "ends" Initiative Objectives as well, typically in reference to timeframes and resources.

Issue. Either 1) a problem that must be solved for which there is not yet a feasible solution, or 2) a decision that must be made about which the relevant decision makers are not in agreement.

Jargon. Words some understand and others do not.

Means. The work undertaken to get to an outcome or destination. In the context of writing decision papers, this is the work done *during* the preparation of the decision paper to develop and finalize the paper.

Mission. Why an organization exists; the outcome it is there to produce.

Objective. A discrete target, the completion of which is usually one step toward the larger goal. It is useful to isolate objectives that, together, will reach a desired goal but are better managed individually.

Risk Management. The assessment and analysis of future possible undesirable states of reality that would impede or prevent the attainment of stated objectives.

Stupid. Communicating, acting, or making decisions without regard to facts or logic. Often, the stupid will insist that their lack of reasoning does not exist or is not important. Often the stupid will pick a position that, when not thought through, seems plausible on its surface to those uninformed about the topic. The opposite of *stupid* is *thoughtful.*

System Objectives. Physical, technical, or discrete end products—such as changes in ongoing policy, organization, process, systems, equipment, or technology.

Teaming. According to Professor Amy Edmondson, "The art of communicating and coordinating with people across boundaries of all kinds—expertise, status, and distance, to name the most important."[21]

Vision. The desired future end state. Vision is defined irrespective of the tasks and the journey that lead to the vision.

White Paper. A document written to promote one organization's product or service to another organization for commercial purposes. A white paper is not a decision paper; it is not a special case of decision paper.

---

[21] Amy Edmondson, *The Fearless Organization: Creating Psychological Safety in the Workplace for Learning, Innovation, and Growth* (Hoboken, New Jersey: John Wiley & Sons, 2019), xv.

Bibliography

Ahn, Woo-Kyoung. *Thinking 101: Why We So Often Get Things Wrong in Life and How We Can All Do Better.* New York: Flatiron Books, 2022.

Bonhoeffer, Dietrich. *Letters and Papers from Prison.* Minneapolis, Minnesota: Fortress Press, 2015.

Edmondson, Amy. *The Fearless Organization: Creating Psychological Safety in the Workplace for Learning, Innovation, and Growth.* Hoboken, New Jersey: John Wiley & Sons, Inc., 2019.

George T. Doran. *There's a S.M.A.R.T. way to Write Management's Goals and Objectives.* New York: Management Review, 1981.

International Organization for Standardization. *Risk Management—Guidelines,* 2nd ed. ISO 31000:2018(en). Paris: ISO, 2018. In English, French, Spanish, and Arabic. https://www.iso.org/obp/ui/en/#iso:std:iso:31000.

Jackson, Maggie. *Uncertain: The Wisdom and Wonder of Being Unsure.* Lanham, Maryland: Rowman & Littlefield Publishing Group, 2023.

Kilpatrick, James J. *The Writer's Art.* Kansas City and New York: Andrews, McMeel & Parker, a Universal Press Syndicate Company, 1984.

Kloman, H. Felix. *The Fantods of Risk: Essays on Risk Management.* Lyme, Connecticut: Seawrack Press, Inc., 2008.

Marks, Norman. *World-Class Risk Management.* Self-published, CreateSpace, 2015.

Renn, Ortwin. *Risk Governance: Coping with Uncertainty in a Complex World.* London: Earthscan, 2008.

Seidman, Dov. *How: Why How We Do Anything Means Everything.* Hoboken, New Jersey: John Wiley & Sons, Inc., 2007.

Tufte, Edward Rolf. *Envisioning Information.* Cheshire, Connecticut: Graphics Press, 1990.

Tufte, Edward Rolf. *The Visual Display of Quantitative Information.* Cheshire, Connecticut: Graphics Press, 1983.

Tufte, Edward Rolf. *Visual Explanations.* Cheshire, Connecticut: Graphics Press, 1997.

Zinsser, William. *On Writing Well, 30th Anniversary Edition.* New York: Collins, 2006.

Zinsser, William. *Writing to Learn.* New York: Harper & Row Publishers, 1988.

About the Author

Erwin Martinez is a seasoned Information Technology executive with over 42 years of experience in writing and coaching others on creating impactful business documents. His extensive career includes 24 years as a Chief Information Officer (CIO), 3 years as an IT director, and 15 years in information systems consulting.

Erwin has published numerous articles on IT management, project management, and the board of directors' role in governance oversight of IT. Known for his hands-on approach, he has been deeply involved in the creation of business decision papers—documents designed to effect major changes, solve problems, and drive strategic initiatives. He has authored, reviewed, and presented these papers to executive teams, CEOs, and boards, often overseeing the implementation of their recommendations.

His insights and methodologies have shaped countless business strategies and decisions, making him a trusted advisor and thought leader in IT and business management. Having coached many professionals on writing effective business decision papers, this book was born out of his desire to create a universally accessible guide to business writing that anyone can use to achieve success.

Index

www.ingramcontent.com/pod-product-compliance
Lightning Source LLC
Chambersburg PA
CBHW071715140626
46557CB00011B/500